M000043189

PENGUIN BOOKS
AMEN

Born in 1956 in Thrissur, Kerala, Meamy Raphael, later Sister Jesme, was the fourth child of her parents. She completed her school and college education in Thrissur and Palakkad. In June 1974, she started her religious training, but with special sanction, was permitted to continue higher studies for M. Phil. and Ph.D on a merit scholarship of the Government of India. Since 1980, she has been teaching, by turns, at two Catholic colleges in Thrissur; she was Vice-Principal at one and Principal at the other, for three years each. Jesme left the Congregation of Mother of Carmel in August 2008, while applying for voluntary retirement from service in the college.

AMEN

The Autobiography of a Nun

Sister Jesme

PENGUIN BOOKS

PENGUIN BOOKS
Published by the Penguin Group
Penguin Books India Pvt. Ltd, 11 Community Centre, Panchsheel Park,
New Delhi 110 017, India
Penguin Group (USA) Inc., 375 Hudson Street, New York, New York 10014, USA
Penguin Group (Canada), 90 Eglinton Avenue East, Suite 700, Toronto,
Ontario, M4P 2Y3, Canada (a division of Pearson Penguin Canada Inc.)
Penguin Books Ltd, 80 Strand, London WC2R 0RL, England
Penguin Ireland, 25 St Stephen's Green, Dublin 2, Ireland
(a division of Penguin Books Ltd)
Penguin Group (Australia), 250 Camberwell Road, Camberwell,
Victoria 3124, Australia (a division of Pearson Australia Group Pty Ltd)
Penguin Group (NZ), 67 Apollo Drive, Rosedale, North Shore 0632, New Zealand
(a division of Pearson New Zealand Ltd)
Penguin Group (South Africa) (Pty) Ltd, 24 Sturdee Avenue, Rosebank,
Johannesburg 2196, South Africa

Penguin Books Ltd, Registered Offices: 80 Strand, London WC2R 0RL, England

First published by Penguin Books India 2009

Copyright © Dr Sister Jesme 2009

10 9 8 7 6 5 4 3 2 1

ISBN 9780143067085

For sale in the Indian Subcontinent only

The views and opinions expressed in this book are the author's own and the facts are as
reported by her which have been verified to the extent possible, and the publishers are
not in any way liable for the same.

Typeset in Adobe Garamond by SÜRYA, New Delhi
Printed at Gopsons Papers Ltd, Noida

CONTENTS

ACKNOWLEDGEMENTS

This is just an attempt to disclose the hitherto hidden life inside the enclosures of the convents. In my own humble way, but empowered by Lord Jesus Himself, my aim is solely the reformation of the Church; to enable society to have a peep into the panoramic but veiled ocean, like the seashell that holds a few drops of sea water. So that the book should in no way hurt those inside the *iron curtain*, unlike in an autobiography, I have purposely used fictitious names. Let the fresh breeze enter the closed walls and purify its stinking corners. May the Holy Spirit liberate the chained souls in the dungeon-like interior of the Holy Abode.

Though the book was first published in Malayalam, I had initially written it in English and I wanted it to be published in that language. Once during Mass I asked Jesus, 'When will *Amen* be published in English?' When I came home, I got phone calls from *Times Now* and *Aaj Tak* as they wanted to interview me. Soon other channels—NDTV, CNN, NEWS X, and many more from Mumbai and Delhi—contacted me. Later, there were interviews from Hong Kong and London via video-conferencing and live interviews from different channels.

Could Jesus have heard my prayer so swiftly? On the heels of this coverage, English publishers approached me, one after another, and I was obliged to seek legal counsel. After negotiations, I selected Penguin Books India.

This new edition, with ample additions and changes, targets a wide range of readers in and outside the country. It has been made more comprehensible to those who are not familiar with the present scenario of the Church in Kerala. The book has benefited much from the comments of my well-wishers as well as that of the Church, and their suggestions have been addressed in this edition. There is a long line of those who deserve due commendation and my deepest gratitude.

I wish to thank:

—Penguin Books India, especially Sri Ravi Singh, Smt. Kamini Mahadevan and Sri Dileepraj for their generosity and commitment to bettering the socio–literary–spiritual–intellectual arena of the country by publishing relevant books, as well as for their personal dedication in the editing and publishing of this particular book;

—the intimate and sincere friends who remain steadfastly with me, especially in times of trouble and restraints, along with the multitudes of students and co-workers, admirers and beneficiaries;

—my family and relatives who were supporting me for quite a long time, and encouraging me;

—the authorities and the teachers, and my colleagues in the Church and the Congregation who helped me to bud and bloom in the Garden of Jesus;

—to all the readers of this book who will assuredly join hands with me in the regaining of the Faith Vision among the believers, leading to the renovation of the Church;

—to all my foes who continue to throw stones at me, misunderstanding the vision of Jesus I seek to accomplish through *Amen*;

—above all, to my beloved Spouse, *Jesus Christ* and His loving *Mother Mary*.

Kozhikode,   SR JESME
April 2009

AUTHOR'S NOTE

What has inspired me to pen this memoir, after spending thirty-three long years in the convent? It is an exceptional step. But for me, it is a journey of passing from one significant phase of my life to another, like the train travel from Delhi to Ernakulam, which has swept me along. There were friends to help me but the decision to leave was only mine. Travelling alone, with Jesus, my beloved Lord as my beacon, I escaped from a Formidable Fortress to His Safe Anchorage.

In this moment of inner turmoil and turbulence all around, writing provides a cathartic relief and a space for self-reflection. It exercises the mind and is also a spiritual activity. It will help launch me onto the next phase of my life, which now stands at a crossroad. I seek to learn from all that has happened in my life so far and try to gain wisdom for the future.

To the society around me, I owe it to share my experiences in all their bareness and totality. People around me have the right to know what happens inside the prison-like 'enclosures' in their very midst. Religious authorities teach, guide, interfere, provoke and console, touching practically every aspect of the lives of the people around them. Yet, for most people, the religious world remains mysterious. My repeated question is: Why is so much secrecy created around ordinary things? I believe that the Church should be transparent in its dealings. Why and whom are we afraid of, if we go along Jesus' Way? Unlike personal matters, where privacy should be respected by the media and society, issues relating to society can be shared and discussed. Only when there is injustice, dishonesty or unfair dealings, does the tendency for secrecy arise; but even in social affairs, unnecessary secrecy is detrimental to the good health of the institutions concerned.

Autobiographies like Mahatma Gandhi's *My Experiments with Truth*, Kiran Bedi's *I Dare* and K.J. Alphons's *Making A Difference* offer us an insight into their eventful lives, and this becomes their contribution to society and the next generation. I don't claim to be great, but, hopefully, my experiences will enable society to reach closer to the truth. Moreover, my case today is spoken of alongside those of the late Sr Abhaya and the late Sr Anupa Mary. Both are no longer alive to narrate their experiences. They are now represented by their parents, whose words may or may not be believed. The responsibility to reveal things as they are, then, naturally falls upon me.

I don't claim this to be an autobiography; it is only a revelation of a part of my life. It neither starts at the very beginning nor comes up till the present—the curtain falls when I leave the convent. The river of life flows on; but it is we who try to find a beginning and an end to our narration. Though not a complete presentation of the reality, I can affirm it represents the truth, to the best of my ability and perception.

Once again, I would like to affirm that this is not an attempt to sully the sacred reputation of the Church or the Religious Congregations. I honour and respect the Church, the Head of which is Christ Himself. I bow before the present Respectable Authorities of the Church. As part of sharing my life in the Congregation of Mother of Carmel (CMC), I may have disclosed some of the just and unjust ways I encountered there, but I have not shied away from admitting my failures and weaknesses either. My constant effort has been not to hurt the feelings or tarnish the image of persons I have come across. Most of the names of people and institutions mentioned are different from the original. How can I not remember with due respect and gratitude all those who 'grew me up'? But, I do wish to underline that everything I have described in this book actually happened and is not imagined or hearsay. If Madhavikutty (Kamala Das) can say that she left her religion, taking Lord Krishna with her, I, too, can very well declare that I left the CMC holding the hands of my Spouse Jesus and Mother Mary.

ESCAPE IN DISGUISE
PROLOGUE

The Mangala Express from Delhi to Ernakulam is speeding up. It is a less-crowded compartment. Being the only woman among the passengers here, I am a bit panicky. But that is not the only reason. I am escaping in disguise, dressed in churidar instead of my habit. This journey is different from any before. It is taking me from one significant phase of my life to another: from a life of enclosure to one of exposure; from a spiritual existence inside the boundaries of the convent to a spiritual life outside its gigantic compound walls; from a black-and-white experience of God's beauty to a multicoloured rhapsody of God's diversity and splendour in Nature; from the Pax Romana atmosphere of security to serenity despite the turbulence of open space. My destination is uncertain. Susmitha, my dear old friend, in Kozhikode, has repeatedly told me that her home is always open for me. So have her husband and only son. Many a time I have stayed with Susmitha and her son during my doctoral research at Calicut University, as her husband is working abroad. I feel safer at Susmitha's than at a convent; but I've told the sisters that I am staying at a recruiting house of the foreign sisters. I have let Susmitha know of my final decision to quit the convent; and she and her family have welcomed me wholeheartedly.

My decision to leave comes prior to the Vatican's beatification of Saint Alphonsa, the first Catholic saint from India. The Church in Kerala is ecstatic over this honour of sainthood being bestowed upon one of their own. Cynics declare that the very authorities who put her through the sufferings, and which were presented to the Vatican as evidence for sainthood, are now celebrating her! Ironically, around the time of my leaving, the cases of Sr Abhaya and Sr Anupa Mary also come to light, taking the shine off a bit from the beatification. Sr Abhaya, a junior sister and a pre-degree student, was living at Pius Xth Convent, Kottayam. According to reports, her body was found in the well inside the convent compound. The initial news of a suicide soon gave way to one of murder, reported to have been committed most probably by the inmates. Suspicions were aroused because of the reports of the hostellers, students of the nearby college and the local people. The recent arrest of two priests and a sister by the Central Bureau of Investigation (CBI) of the Government of India, confirm the immoral goings-on there.

Then, at Kollam, Sr Anupa Mary was found to have hanged herself in the convent. Her father, the cook of the local Bishop, accused the convent inmates of ill-treating her, by forcing her to do long hours of menial work; he also complained of his daughter being sexually harassed by a sister.

Throughout my life in the convent, I was misunderstood by

the other sisters, mainly the Superiors. My questioning their decision and actions in the light of the Bible and the teachings of Jesus always irritated them. Sr Honor, the Principal of Amala College, very sympathetically, once remarked that there was no one in the Congregation to clear my genuine doubts. The subsequent attempts to torture me, by threatening to dismiss me from the post of Principal of a college, on the basis of an anonymous letter—a false allegation among many others that were made against me, the authorities' final and determined attempt to have me declared insane and start treatment to make me passive and silent—left me with no other option but to escape from the convent. I would have been the last person to do so in normal circumstances, but despite deep regret, I had to take a strong decision at this critical juncture.

~

'Chechie, where will you get down?' Awakened from my reverie, I stare at the coach attendant in the three-tier AC compartment, not used to a stranger addressing me as 'Chechie' (elder sister). People have so far called me 'Sister'. Now I have to get used to people addressing me differently. Wearing churidar gives me this anonymity. Thanks to a friend who suggested this dress for the journey. 'Let this be a minor defiance on your part,' she advised. In our Congregation, wearing churidar can invite severe punishment. My record of obedience for all these thirty-three years in the convent has been well appreciated. Only by some notable acts of disobedience on my part, will they now be forced to accept my request for leaving. At the moment, my fear is that they will catch me before I can officially, in the presence of witnesses, hand over my request. They may tear off my letter and force me back into the convent, if there is nobody with me. By my leaving, many of their secrets will be lost, besides the tidy sum I get as pay, from funds sanctioned by the University Grants Commission (UGC), and which goes into the convent's common pool. The last time I attempted to leave, the authorities forgave me unconditionally and made me rejoin the convent.

In reply to the attendant, I check my ticket and notice it is marked to Ernakulam, though I had asked for a booking from Nizamuddin to Kozhikode. What Providence is this, I wonder? Anyway, I stammer 'Kozhikode' to him. His concern is to get back the bed sheets that have been supplied.

But to slip away quietly is not that simple. Amma, my mother, calls from Thrissur. She remembers the date of my travel! Someone might have reminded her. Anyhow, I can't lie to her, so I tell her about my going to Susmitha's place in Kozhikode.

Amma starts persuading me to come back. Calling me by my pet name, Memy, she advises me to attend Fr Vattayi's Retreat before taking the final decision, or to serve at Shalom, either at the Retreat Centre or at the Media Centre, where I can continue as a sister. Of course, only the so-called 'goody-goody' nuns are welcome there, not me, I tell her. To put an end to all this, I lie that I have already submitted my letter requesting for Dispensation. The ordeal is over.

When I ring up Susmitha to tell her about my safely boarding the train, and to remind her to meet me at the railway station as I have heavy luggage, she responds with timidity and nervousness. There is construction work in progress at her house, as the second storey is being built, and now it is impossible for her to put me up! I know Susmitha well; she would be the last person to tell me so, especially in an emergency like this. Maybe she has been tutored and coaxed by someone influential.

In fact, when I had called her the day before my journey, I found Susmitha a little nervous. Perhaps it was because of my younger sister's call intimidating her. If none would help me, my sister falsely believed, I might continue to be a nun. But at this point, what am I to do! Where am I to go? My brain is working feverishly. A few phone calls later, my classmate and friend from Ernakulam comes to my rescue. We were together during our doctoral research. A friend in need, indeed!

I inform Susmitha of my change of plans. She is relieved. Then I telephone my friend in Delhi about how God has worked a miracle through her travel agent, who by mistake booked a ticket to Ernakulam instead of Kozhikode! Luckily, the people around me do not follow Malayalam, so they cannot make sense of my desperate phone calls.

I take up the novel *The Godfather*, and immerse myself in reading. It saves me from people's probing and keeps my identity hidden. To spend almost three days and two nights in a train, fearful of being caught, is unbearable. Never did I imagine myself in such a plight. Again my mobile starts ringing. Shocked, I read on the screen the name of Fr Joseph, the priest for whom I have been working in Delhi all these months. My understanding is that he will return from Bangalore only after two days. My escape from Delhi was to take place while he was away. Telling him and leaving was not an option—as my authorities have entrusted me to him, he would have informed them the moment he came to know. And that would have definitely spoilt my plans. 'Ignore the call'—that is the only way for me to avoid his questions right now. I put the mobile on the vibrate mode, so that none around notices the unattended calls.

1

JESUS CALLS

It is the first night of the fifty-two-hour train journey. After an early meal, my fellow passengers are preparing for sleep. But my mind slips back to the days when I received a divine call from my Jesus. It is 1973 and I am a pre-degree student at the prestigious St Maria's College. Like a butterfly, I flit about the college, carefree, with my friends and classmates. My clothes are of the latest fashion, but always modest, with trinkets of matching colour. Even the sisters in college appreciate my attire. Being a topper in studies, I have many friends. Movies and novels are my passion. Many a novel have I finished overnight. Wherever I go, I look around for what novels are available. As I move in decent circles, no porn or soft porn novels come to hand. Horror fiction like Dracula haunts me; heroic characters inspire me.

I love to listen to music. Daily I look up the listing of Akashvani programmes for the day in the newspaper, jot down the entertaining items on a slip of paper and keep it on the radio stand. The items are put under two columns, one marked 'Thiru', an abbreviation for Thiruvananthapuram, and 'Kozhi', a short form for Kozhikode. Seeing this, my father teases me: 'See the Thiru-kozhi (holy hen) has climbed on to the radio stand!' With music in the background, I can study well. The music keeps me fresh and alert, and it also helps to stimulate my mind and come up with new ideas.

As a family, we enjoy going for movies. Father takes us mostly for the second show. Towards the end of the Night Prayer in the family, normally if it is around 9.00, I begin to doze, resting my head on the cot near which I kneel. Then father will ask: 'Who all would like to go for a film? Raise your hands.' My hand goes up first and all start laughing. He promptly rings up the theatre to reserve seats, takes the car out of the car shed and is ready to take us all to the movie. After it gets over, we come to his automobile workshop, Kerala Industrials, considered as one of the best in facilities and services in these parts.

The watchman is roused from his sleep and has to hunt all the hotels still open at this hour, to buy whatever is available to eat. We get back only in the wee hours of the morning. This treat is repeated almost every fortnight. Once we were fortunate to see three movies in a week.

Well-off enough to own the first motorbike in the area, father drives all over the place. Not having a silencer like all other bikes, his vehicle makes a phut-phut noise. We children know from a mile when father is approaching. Family gossip has it, of course wrongly, that once he took Amma on his pillion to a night show, something unheard of in Kerala, which is conservative.

The next day during meals, Amma takes the lead in triggering a discussion on the previous night's film. Naturally, her target is my brothers. 'Didn't you notice what happened to the character played by the actor Ummer, after he defied his father?' 'Think of the sacrifice made by Prem Nazir, the hero. God really rewarded him in the end.' Through this lively talk in which we all participate vigorously, she gives us guidance. She sees this as an occasion to teach us morals. Unlike in some families, we can enjoy worldly pleasures so long as they are moral and lawful. There are no grandparents or elderly people in the house to come in the way of normal entertainment. Father happens to be the youngest son among his family, married at the age of twenty-one; so also Amma, the youngest in her family, and married at the age of fifteen.

We are seven siblings, three brothers and four sisters, with me being the fourth child, the middle one—the eldest, third and sixth children are boys, the rest of us girls. At home, democracy rather than strict hierarchy prevails; mother respects the opinion of even the youngest child, if it is sensible, whatever the matter. It is a loving and lively atmosphere at home.

My school, St Joseph's Latin Convent, a branch of St Theresa's Ernakulam, is opposite our home and, even before I join there, my family frequent it and we often play there. Barely two, I am taken to act as Baby Jesus in a school function. The nuns and teachers have to hold me from below to keep me from wobbling off the platform! At the age of three, I am sent to a nursery (there was no LKG/UKG then) and remain there, unusually, for almost three years.

So when it is time to formally join school, I don't know why, but I feel like a princess among the other girls! That feeling remains right up to eighth standard. I get a double promotion to second standard, but then, much to my dismay, my father insists that I repeat third standard, otherwise I would be too young when the time came to appear for the SSLC examination. I sing and dance at the drop of a hat and am always in demand to perform in various items at school functions. How I used to long at times to sit among the audience so that I can watch and enjoy others perform!

In fourth standard, I play the villainous role of a boy, Plum, in a school play. The characters, named after fruits, are to plant roses and present them to the Queen, and the best roses win a prize. Mischievous Plum is lazy and tries to present the Queen with an artificial rose, which is perfect and far more beautiful than the real one. He is about to get the prize when his trick is discovered and he is punished instead. My father later explains the moral of the story to me—never to cheat in order to get something.

Despite enjoying many such simple pleasures, even then there is a spiritual and mystical pull within me towards Jesus. Amma's piety as well as some of the nuns' exemplary lives and preaching has also aroused my love for Jesus. Amma's frequent fasting and prayer is little known outside the family. A neighbour, who has seen her at a window sipping something from a glass, swiftly decides it can only be liquor. The gossip going around is that, scandalously, she occasionally joins my father for a glass when he drinks. Only much later do people realize, to their shame, that she has been soothing her parched throat with plain water while fasting!

Sr Michel, the class sister of fifth and sixth standards, narrates stories of saints and infant Jesus in class. I play at giving sermons about Jesus to imaginary people around me. Ascending to the top of the steps leading to our toilets, I hold forth on Biblical themes. Amma, watching this from the window of the kitchen, encourages me to continue. My one hobby is to narrate stories about Jesus to my younger brother and sisters. These are not from the Bible but rather parables made up by people about the divine love of Jesus. One story is about a motherless boy who longs to see his dead mother.

By chance, the door of a room in the house with Jesus on the Cross is left ajar one day and the boy goes in and begs Jesus to show him his mother. Jesus asks the boy whether he will come along and be ready to die, if He takes him to her. The boy is overjoyed, even as Jesus pierces him with the nail in His bleeding hand, and leads him across to his mother in Heaven. What a powerful, though dark, story, enough to leave anybody wonderstruck, let alone a child.

From childhood, Jesus has been beside me. Every evening, there is a family prayer, from about 8 to 9 o'clock. Almost daily, we attend Mass that usually starts around 6.15 or 6.30 in the morning. The church is across the road from our house. Amma does not miss a day, but sometimes we are slow in getting ready and reach there only at the tail end of the Mass, when some people are returning! After Mass and tiffin, we are off to school, at 9.30.

When I am about seven, it is time for my First Confession and First Holy Communion. These sacraments are a landmark in any Catholic's life. I am doubly happy because I can skip school that day! And then, I will get to wear a pretty white dress and a delicate lace veil, almost like a bride. At the shop, I am shown a white veil sprinkled with glitter and another one with pretty embroidered flowers and edged with lace. When asked to choose, I want to take both, as they are so pretty! Father teases me that at my First Confession, I will have to tell the priest about my greediness! The family cossets and fusses over me. On the day of the Holy Communion—this follows that of the First Confession—my mother bathes me, carries me, rather than leading me to the bedroom, and herself dresses me in the white dress, stockings and pretty white shoes. From first standard onwards, I attend the catechism class at Sunday school in church. Unconsciously, Jesus has been growing within and alongside me as my beloved Friend and Companion.

Finishing high school, I move to college. During the second year of the pre-degree course, there is a compulsory Retreat for all the Catholic students. It is called the 'Closed Retreat' as students have to stay in the college for its duration of three days. Somehow, I do not like this idea, as I believe that one cannot reap a good spiritual harvest from a Retreat conducted by a college. Though prejudiced, I still go and join my Catholic friends there. My only aim is to have a good time with them. But then the preacher and his utterances at the Retreat appeal to me as being genuine.

'Jesus will walk these three days amidst you all. Like the dwarfish Zaccheus, if you have an ardent desire to meet Him, He will call you by name and come to your heart to dine with you.' Oh! What a consoling thought. Many of us take it in the real spirit and wait earnestly to meet Him face to face. The priest assures us: 'I may be the last prophet from Heaven sent to redeem you. If you don't repent and return to Him now, there may never be another chance for you.' His words reverberate in the depth of our minds as God's own revelation through this prophet. There is pin-drop silence. Everyone is moved by these pronouncements. For the first time in my life, I begin seriously to think about my future. My decision to give up reading novels, to combat the unquenchable thirst for the latest in clothes and fashion and the yearning for worldly pleasures, is the outcome of these three days. But the climactic surrender occurs only during the final hours of the Retreat.

Almost all of us are in the auditorium-cum-chapel even hours before the concluding Mass. After praying to Virgin Mary to help me choose my vocation, I turn to my beloved Jesus for an intimate talk. Almost in a trance, I spend an hour in His presence. What a lovely and sweet experience! Towards the end, I hear Him distinctly asking, 'Memy, won't you give your whole heart to me?' It is an invitation for total surrender. My love for Him is so deep that I want to say 'YES', but am held back by the thoughts of worldly attractions. I argue, dissent, whine, retort, plead, explain, justify, and what not! His request is repeated until I surrender, though initially, I put forth many conditions that He be near me and assist me.

The Holy Mass seems to be a divine banquet where Jesus, my Spouse, receives me as His bride. After the Holy Communion, during the ecstatic union between us, He places a ring on my finger, proclaiming me as His Own. Spiritually, I am raised to the Heavens and I realize that I can only be His. No more marriage for me. No more worldliness. He is my only refuge, my rock, my fortress, my way, my truth, my salvation, my joy—my everything.

The vote of thanks is given to Father this time not just by one girl, as is usual, but many who jump onto the stage to thank him. Everyone is touched by the divine experience. Alice comes towards me suddenly: 'Memy, why don't you go up to the stage and share your experience?' I refuse. 'Is it because you don't like the Retreat?' she asks. I am silent, though I want to tell her that my experience is beyond description. Words can never convey its true meaning. Gradually, she will come to know of my transformation. Then my silence will be eloquent for all around. My travel back home gives me a chance to practise abstinence. In a Kerala State Road Transport Corporation (KSRTC) bus, crowded with men and women, I dive into my secret recess, clasping the palms of Jesus.

When I reach home, my brothers and sisters gather around me, curious about my experiences. Describing only peripheral events, the stories the preacher narrated and the passages he read out, I withdraw to the other room, to be by myself. That night, unable to sleep, I go to Amma and wake her up. To avoid disturbing the others who are asleep, we go to the dining room for a heart-to-heart talk. It is then that I reveal my real experience with the Lord, His special call and my wholehearted surrender to Him. Amma says: 'Molé, this may be transient. Your sudden decision may not be the right one. After attending prayer sessions, even I used to wish to become a nun. But it is all fanciful thinking.'

'Amma, I, too, have had similar experiences before. But this is different. I have given my word to Him,' I tell her. She cautions, 'Memy, it is better not to tell anyone else about this. Not even your brothers. They won't stop teasing you once they get to know.' She also tells me about the two letters she has just received from my chechie at Chanda, a mission centre in Madhya Pradesh. Chechie, after her B.Sc., has gone with the CMC sisters to the mission area, as a teacher in a school run by the sisters but managed by the ACC cement factory. She is living with the sisters in their convent, attending all the prayer services, and sharing everything with them. And she is quite happy too. But then, to everyone's surprise, she sends them a letter expressing her desire to join the convent. We know how she loves fashions and style and will never think of a lifestyle that would involve sacrificing all that. We are relieved by the letter that follows, the same day, explaining that her first letter was written at the persuasion of the Superior, who loves her very much, and the second letter is the one which actually reflects her opinion. In this second letter, mailed without the knowledge of the Superior, she clarified that she does not wish to join the convent at all. My mother says: 'See God's mysterious ways! My eldest daughter doesn't want to join the convent, despite the compulsion. My second daughter decides to become a nun, even though nobody wants her to be so.' Now we return to our own beds.

The pre-degree first year results are expected the next day. Usually, I will be very tense and nervous. But this time, I am cool on reaching the college. As it turns out, I have scored the highest marks in the Arts group in the college and my friends are overjoyed. Later, I am awarded the gold medal for Catechism. I smile and look at my Jesus in my heart. The Holy Masses I attend afterwards become occasions to renew my vow to Him. But no one suspects the transformation I have undergone. Not even my intimate friends. I keep wearing stylish clothes, accompany my family for movies, listen to music and dance at home, as I used to before. Including Amma, nobody at home has noticed the change within me.

Towards the end of my pre-degree course, we have great financial troubles at home. There are times when Amma finds it difficult to give me the monthly fees. Dad is not bothered at all about these things. Even the scholarship money I get throughout for my studies is used to meet household expenses. Bishop Kundukulam had been our family counsellor when he was a parish priest. This relationship continues even after he becomes the Bishop. He assures my mother that in this crisis, should she need help, especially in remitting my fees, we can turn to him. There are two occasions when Amma tells me to go to the Bishop's House for the fees. It is so humiliating for me to go past St Thomas College, enduring students' arrows that accompany their 'words of honey', and avoiding the stares of the priests in the Bishop's House, as I climb up the stairs towards the Bishop's room. Seeing me, the Bishop comes out and hands me an envelope containing fifteen rupees and fifty paisa, the exact amount for the fees; and I run down the stairs and dash to the college, without a word of 'thanks' to him. This ordeal is repeated once more during the academic year. But for Jesus, it would be hard to bear this shame.

The pre-degree second year exams are over and it is time to reveal my decision to all. Amma says, 'Molé, you haven't forgotten? I didn't know you still have such a desire.'

'Because you told me not to tell anybody, I have kept quiet so far, Amma. But each day, I have been renewing my promise to Him. I can't live without Him, Amma.' On learning that I am leaving home forever, my dad starts crying, my *cheriangala* (brother just elder to me) begins shouting and my chechie asks me why. But Amma who had hoped I would change my mind, sighs and says: 'God claims the best one among my children. To Him, one should give the middle [the choicest] piece of the fish. I can't refuse Him anything.'

At this, chechie intervenes, expressing doubt about my unexpected decision. As far as she knows, there is none in our *tharavad* (family-clan) who has joined a convent. Our tharavad is well known for merry-making, revelry, feasting and so on. Even before all can disperse after a family function, we will be discussing the next get-togethers, marriages and ceremonies in the larger family. Never has anyone spoken of spiritual things, let alone about joining the nunnery or seminary. It is true that in my house too, in spite of all the devotion and prayer, a life in religion is never thought of or discussed. Such a life, we've believed, is destined for special people, born in particular families.

And then, what do I really know about a nun's life?

So far, I have not bothered to find out about the sisters' way of life. I wonder, 'Can they laugh aloud? Are they allowed to have innocent pleasures?' I even have a serious doubt which appears to be funny to the others. Once I asked Amma: 'How much pain do the sisters endure when they undergo the operation to remove their breasts?' and she laughed aloud: 'Haven't you noticed Sr Georgia's chest?' I have never observed as there was no reason to. My understanding is that breasts are of no use for nuns, so why keep them? I want to join the convent only for the sake of Jesus. Only because He chose me; called me; promised to be with me.

But now that I have decided to become a sister, I have some basic questions. Do the nuns live according to the will of Jesus? Do they feel duped after entering the convent? Are they genuinely happy and satisfied? I decide to find out about all this from Sr Pushpam Chechie, a distant relative, who I believe will tell me the truth. But now my own chechie is here, ready to answer my queries. Though she tries to dissuade me from this harsh decision, she clears all my doubts, as she has been with the sisters in the mission areas. When she realizes that I am firm on my decision to join the vocation, she starts talking seriously. I am in a quandary as to which congregation to join. The priest at the Syrian Church, some distance away, is not that close to us; so we can't turn to him for advice. We attended the Latin Church, which was across the road from us—also perhaps because the Mass was less formal—until we were told by the Syrian Church fathers to come there. Now chechie comes to my assistance. The motto of the Congregation of Mother of Carmel is 'Contemplation and Action', she says. 'Memy, you may like their motto. Pray and find out God's will; then put it into action. When you are exhausted, go and get spiritual strength from the Lord. Igniting your torch from Him, go to the field of work again.' I am impressed. I feel the Lord is speaking through my chechie; she cannot be wrong. The Lord's path is becoming clear for me. Amma takes me to the Principal of my college for guidance. A very motherly sister she is. She is amazed at the way Jesus works. 'Are girls suddenly getting into such vocations even in this day and age?' she asks. Following her advice, we proceed to St Antony's Convent. The sisters there inform me that I should come when the school reopens in June and join them as a nursery teacher.

Close relatives come to know of my decision and respond with shock, sympathetic comments, accusing arrows, and the like. 'She is very selfish, running away from the troubles of life. This is a sort of escapism,' one of my aunts comments. 'What unusual things are happening in your house? You will be the second nun in our tharavad. The first one joined some twenty-five years back. Who knows whether she is alive or not!' remarks another aunt. This implies that they never visit or enquire after a family member once she or he chooses the religious life. What an attitude! I, too, can expect only something similar after I join.

Any girl who wishes to join the convent should attend a Vocation Retreat. There the preacher, a priest, describes to us the two ways of life—married and religious—after which we may decide. At the interview thereafter, the priest guides us about which path we may follow. Those who have chosen the religious life are asked to live in a boarding, adjacent to a convent. You are assigned duties like teaching, or serving in a hospital, by the authorities. Daily you should attend Mass, recite the rosary, Novena (special prayer recited to some saints, or to Mother Mary or St Joseph), and so on. This is the period when they observe us and see whether we are fit for the religious life. We, too, can reflect and find out if we can live up to it. During this time, the sisters will be very loving towards us.

Packing my bag with things necessary for a nursery teacher, I reach the convent. It is June 1974. My pre-degree exam results are not out as yet. I am to be a boarder for almost a year. Leaving home for the first time is an issue, but my love for Jesus makes me go. Even at this point, my family has taken me to see *The Sound of Music*, hoping that I would be swayed by the film and follow the example of Maria, who quits the convent and marries the count, whose children she looks after as a nanny!

Besides the sarees for school wear, I have taken long skirts and blouses to wear after teaching hours. But I am instructed to dress at least in a half-saree (a full-length skirt and blouse, over which a thin upper cloth is draped) after class hours, so that I look like a teacher to the children in the orphanage. In the class, my motherly instincts are aroused as I am surrounded by smart, mischievous children. What I have never done so far in my home, I now do gladly, for the sake of my Jesus. The thirty children need to go to the toilet during class hours. I am instructed to get the help of an orphan girl who is in Class IX, at such times. To call her from the classroom upstairs is a problem. How can I leave my other students who may at any time run to the gate and reach the road? We have no security guard here. Besides, I cannot make a younger girl do all this lowly work while I pose as a teacher. I decide to relieve her of this duty. Whoever has a need is taken to the toilet outside the classroom, cleaned, and, if necessary, her knickers are washed. Sweeping the room, and mopping it twice a day is also part of my job.

The pre-degree second year results are awaited eagerly; my

repeated prayer is, 'Sacred Heart of Jesus, I place my trust in You.' And how generous He is in His blessings! I secure the highest marks ever in the Arts group at college. 'You have kept Your word,' I look at Jesus gratefully. I should be happy but this is not to be as yet.

Urged by my college Principal, I seek admission for the degree course in another college, but end up being snubbed. I cannot afford the expenses for the application. My mother's pleading that I have got the highest marks in my college and may please be admitted, is met by the Principal's retort, 'Highest marks? Do you know from how many universities students come here? These will not be very good marks compared to theirs.' Her sneering tone makes Amma come to my defence. 'She has decided to join the convent.' All it invites is a boomerang of a reply: 'This is yet another trick played by people to get admission.' This pierces my heart unlike all the previous arrows. Someone thinking that I am out to deceive them by pretending to have a vocation! How can I prove my genuineness? But somehow, permission is granted and I join the degree course for economics but later change to English literature. I have topped the admission lists both in economics and English.

Though I have gained admission, my yearning to become a sister gets stronger by the day. The religious authorities find a way out to overcome this wait. I can become an Aspirant and continue my studies at Daya College, Palakkad. To the interview for Aspirancy, conducted by the Mother Provincial and her Councillors along with the Vocation Promoter (a sister appointed by the authorities to scout for and encourage girls to join the convent), I have worn a skirt and blouse, and look tiny. Naturally, the Mother Provincial asks: 'You are the fourth in the family and your chechie has not yet married. What made you join the convent in such a hurry?' I reply, 'I want to run to Him, leaving the water pot there itself, like how the Samaritan woman in the Bible did, the moment she recognized Jesus to be her Saviour.' Loud laughter follows from the sisters.

On the day of the ceremony for entering the Aspirancy, we wear white sarees and go for Mass during which we consecrate ourselves to Jesus through special prayers. After the Mass we are welcomed by the authorities, the Aspirant Mistress, and all the other sisters in the refectory (dining hall). After a few days, we are sent to different convents for work. We can wear coloured sarees. The Mistress visits us in our convents often, and on important feast days, we are invited to the Provincial House for group gatherings comprising group prayer, discussions, evaluation, and the like. Towards the end of one year, we assemble in the Provincial House and stay there for a few days in prayer. Then we are sent home awaiting selection for Postulancy. In my case, as an Aspirant, I am to spend two years at Daya College to complete my studies and go to the next stage in the religious training. I start to count the days before I can resume my spiritual training.

Daya College turns out to be a paradise on earth. I end up being there for two years as a full-time student and Aspirant. It is a homely and conducive environment for genuine teaching and learning, with good friends, motherly teachers, simple students and caring hostel wardens. The degree students are the senior-most and are given due respect by the pre-degree students who should call us chechie.

During recreation time, after dinner, the degree students in the hostel form a gang, and they are permitted to pass comments or pull the legs of the juniors. I engage in all the decent revelries, participating in the various hostel competitions and bagging prizes, and once even receiving a cash prize in an essay competition conducted by the Carmelites of Mary Immaculate (CMI) fathers. There I make numerous friends—the rich and poor, the smart and weak, the naughty and saintly; these, as well as the sweepers and toilet cleaners.

As an Aspirant, I am under the charge of a warden mistress who counsels me for a few days. Only on Sundays there is a mandatory hour of spiritual reading, though I am expected to attend Mass every day, which I do between 6.00 and 6.30 in the morning, before going for classes. On Good Friday I decide to undertake a 'whole fast', taking nothing but one and a half glasses of water for the entire day. This is really tough as the fast starts after supper the previous day and goes on until breakfast the day after, with work or studies continuing alongside. It is more trying than the normal fast before any feast and on first Fridays of each month. All this is good training for the disciple to follow on becoming a sister. Then, in the normal fast, we are allowed to have black coffee but no breakfast after morning Mass, a full lunch, black coffee in the evening, and a supper of *kanji* with one curry. On other days, for supper there is usually rice and more than one curry. On Good Friday, as a symbol of mourning, there is no breakfast, only lunch with rice and mango curry, and you must kneel while eating.

It is also the period of the Charismatic Renewal. This is a

general movement in the twentieth century for change in the Church. It took some time to spread in Kerala as the medium of the prayer services had to be changed to Malayalam. The tradition-minded priests and nuns are against this movement, which is more liberal and democratic in outlook and methods of prayer services. There is active involvement of ordinary people which has lessened the monopoly of the clergy in many of the prayer programmes. Here God is seen as being more loving and considerate. In our Retreat, the preaching is in English, not as expected in Malayalam, and only those who can follow the language have the privilege of attending it. Our core group, headed by a staff member, prays and toils hard to bring a well-known Charismatic Leader, Rev. Fr Fio Mascarenhas, to our college. This Retreat and the prayer sessions deepen my bond with the Lord.

But there is another, unsavoury, aspect of college life. The college hostel is notorious for homosexual friendship. My understanding is that this is because the hostellers rarely meet boys about the campus. Naturally, the craze for romance at that age takes the wrong path and ends up in their own gender. I have seen some undesirable scenes where a chechie and *anujathie* (younger sister) are entwined. 'It is none of my business,' I tell myself. Some moms even send gifts to such chechies, without knowing that they are spoiling the studies as well as the future of their daughters. Of course, such happenings also give room for imaginations to run wild!

In my final year, the daughter of a doctor is admitted to the pre-degree course. She happens to be the prettiest girl in the college. All eyes are turned on her whenever she comes out of her room in the hostel. Invariably, she has a couple of girl admirers hanging around her. One day, the pretty girl's (let me call her Pretty) friends come running to me with a gold ring and ask me to hide it. 'Memychechie, Pretty has left it in the bathroom and has forgotten; let her search for it for a while. When she comes to you, give it back to her only after some questioning.' It is meant to be a prank, so I agree and play along. Many a time, I allow the other girls to play such silly but harmless tricks. Once Pretty brings me a gift—a glittering crucifix. Refusing to accept, I send it back to her. Next week, she sends it by parcel post. During a residential camp conducted by the All India Catholic Universities Federation (AICUF), she declares that she has decided to join the convent. Her inclination towards convent life perhaps explains her noticing me. Gradually, we become thick friends. It is genuine and sincere amity. Her family comes to visit me too. Amma also loves her. Everything is fine until Pretty leaves for the Revision holidays while I am still in the hostel. Now things take an ugly turn.

Pretty sends me a box of photos of her aunty from America and her family, along with a jasmine garland she had made and a letter giving details of the enclosed photos, through her neighbour, who comes to college for exams. After viewing them, I hand back the box to that girl along with my reply, when by chance the Superintendent Sister sees it lying around on a sill and confiscates and locks it up in her cupboard. I get to know about this through an attender girl. The Superintendent keeps this as evidence against my good conduct. The hostel maid has also popped into the box a stupid note about Pretty and me, which I had taken as a joke. But now this is regarded as a blot on my religious life. I feel helpless. Pretty wants the photos back before her aunty returns. Her parents ring up the Sister but she denies hiding the box. I am distraught.

I cannot concentrate and prepare for my last university exam. If my religious life is at stake, I don't want to complete my studies. Only out of obedience to the authorities did I join the degree course. If I am not fit to enter the convent, I am not interested in anything else. My new life's ambition stares back at me. Sharing my sorrow with my warden sister-mistress would be a relief, but she is far away at a Retreat. Meanwhile, my friends have come to know of my plight and they help me to prepare by reading aloud the lessons. Half awake, half dozing I listen to their voices.

The next day, as I reach the exam hall my teacher-sister asks: 'Memy, what happened to you? You look as if you are coming from the grave.' I burst out crying. Only with all her reassurance am I able to make it to the examination hall when the long bell rings. It is the worst exam in my life. When I disclose everything that has happened to the sister, she takes it up with the Superintendent Sister, who denies everything. My teacher-sister's intervention saves me from further enquiries and punishments, though I never get the photos back, and Pretty's aunty leaves for America without them. I return home with Amma and await permission from the convent authorities to pursue my religious training. But I am destined to wait a little longer.

I soon receive a call from the authorities to be a teacher in a parallel college run by the CMC sisters, as part of the training. This is wonderful for me. Teaching the pre-degree students turns out to be a thrilling experience. Many of the girls are from the nearby village of Parapur; they are poor and weak students, and hardly have any exposure. Their getting so far is an achievement in itself. Of course, they don't know any English.

My degree results are expected any day. I recall the worst exam I ever wrote and hope for a miracle. I had been aiming for a university rank, but that seems like a daydream now. Or is it? A friend comes and tells me that I have stood second in the English literature degree exams. The college rejoices, because for years it has not received a university rank in that particular discipline. But the reaction of my students leaves me stumped. They have only read of rank holders in the papers so far—so few were they—and now they are awestruck to see one in flesh and blood! My eyes and heart are raised to Him in inexplicable joy. 'Jesus! You did it!'

By evening, Mother Provincial and the Assistant Provincial, later the Superior General, come to congratulate me and to request me to continue my studies for postgraduation at Amala College where I did my pre-degree. I begin pleading with them to let me become a nun first. 'Haven't I been waiting for all these three years? Didn't I obey all that you have told me so far? This time spare me please . . .' Understanding my feelings, they reply: 'All right, you pray and let us know what Jesus tells you. We have revealed our decision.' The whole day I spend in prayer and meditation. In the end, I bow to their will.

Once again, I am with my former batch in Amala. The year is 1977 and I will be there for two years. I am fortunate that a new rule has come into force. From then on, Aspirants may stay inside the convent along with all the other sisters. My happiness is beyond words! Ceremoniously, I enter the enclosure of the convent, after years of waiting. Attending some of the prayer services with the nuns, having food in the same refectory, sleeping under the same roof, I come into closer contact with them. Almost all the sisters there form pairs. They walk, eat, work, go for recreation together, and, for bathing, even go up till the bathroom together. Without the support of a partner, it is difficult to manage there. If you are sick, or go without food, only the partner will take care of you.

Every convent has a chapel, a refectory and living rooms. The parlour and the chapel are accessible to outsiders, but the rest of the place is considered as the enclosure. The chaplain can enter the enclosure, except the living rooms. Each CMC sister has to be provided with a single cubicle, even if it is separated by sheets of cloth. The servants from outside can come to the kitchen and working area. Every convent has a garden. Flowers are needed for Mass, and other prayer services.

As Aspirants, or even later as Postulants and Novices, we have little to do by way of everyday chores of running the convent. We see little of the sisters, who do all the manual jobs. These are women who join the convent in their girlhood, committing themselves for lifelong service to the Lord; less-educated and belonging to the poorer sections of society, they remain *cheduthies* or elevated servants throughout their lives. Many of them are dissatisfied, grumbling about their predicament of neither belonging fully to the convent nor the family. Only those who remain virgin are allowed to continue in the convent. When they die, the cheduthies have the privilege of a religious funeral service and of being buried in the same place as the sisters. Prayer services offered for nuns after death is also the right of this section of sisters. These women are often real gems, in their kindness and caring; I always believe that these cheduthies reach Heaven faster than the nuns; or perhaps the nuns are to be recommended by them so as to enter the portals of the other world!

There are many junior sisters here attending college. Unlike at Daya College, here we do not have a sister-mistress to guide us. What a mischievous gang they are! One sister buys sweets and compels me and the other juniors to have them, whether we want to or not. It is another matter that I have a sweet tooth and don't mind! The student-sisters are to sit up until 11 p.m. in the parlour, waiting for the sisters in the college office to come back, after which the main door is locked. It is then that the naughty juniors get into the act! They open the locked cupboard with a nail, and help themselves to biscuits, wafers and any other eatables stored there. Boiled eggs, kept in the fridge, are also stolen sometimes.

But, sometimes, there are also minor sexual aberrations that take place between some student-sisters. The Rule of Touch, along with the Rule of Silence and the Rule of Sight, is very strict in the convent. No sister may touch another. But there are sisters, who sitting beside each other, play 'footsie', as one sister entwines her foot with the other's and rubs against it; or sometimes a sister's hand lingers and caresses another's shoulder, on the pretext of smoothing her dress. These are only a few—and hopefully, stray—instances.

But to my dismay, there are nuns who behave contrary to my

expectations. One senior nun, who is my teacher, avoids long hours of prayer that are laid down for the monthly Recollection Day. Held on the second Saturday of every month, this is a day of prayer and reflection with a view to renewing the Community. There are talks and discussions, and the Service of Reconciliation. The Superior introduces and speaks on a theme for some time. Then each one gets up and, in a general way, discusses her failings in conduct relating to this theme, and asks for the pardon of Jesus and the Community. The idea is self-purification for spiritual advancement. The principle of this observance is good, but many times it is not practised. To my amazement, this senior sister spends that prayer time in cleaning her room, rearranging her possessions, sleeping and washing clothes, which are to be done only during recess hours. Another sister in the office privately studies for the BA course. She wants me to secretly teach her. We hide on a small terrace during the coaching hours.

Groupism is another ill that I did not expect to find here. One cannot live in peace without joining one of the groups. At least that group will save you from the onslaught of the one against you. Somehow, I try to please both the groups, not siding with either, for the sake of my peaceful existence here. When the time comes for the senior sisters to evaluate my conduct, I am fortunate to get a high grade as I have pleased both sides. Another sister makes me write scripts for plays to be staged. Thus, I get involved in almost all the activities of the convent.

Awaiting the final result of my master's, I join the Postulancy, the next step in becoming a nun. I have to bid goodbye to all at home and the other relatives, to my plants and pets, because we can never come back to live at home hereafter. We have to take to the convent all that is in the long list given to us by the authorities. This is the time we should donate patrimony (like a dowry), which is, of course, much less in amount than a dowry.

During the six months of Postulancy, we are taught a little of the Bible, Theology, CMC Constitution, recitation of prayer, etc. Then we begin to participate in Canonical Prayers like Sapra (morning prayer), Ramsa (evening prayer) and Leliya (night prayer). We have to take turns in leading the prayer, or as choir leader, in starting a song, followed by the group. We are also trained in preparing for Mass, Adoration and other prayer services. Besides, we have duties in the garden, kitchen and library, among others. Occasionally, in connection with major feasts, we have cultural programmes in which we wear costumes and dance, act and sing. There are sports competitions too.

Being involved in spiritual matters, I am happy and at peace. I am also pleased to learn informally from my classmate, whose cousin is in the board of postgraduate examinations, that I have come second in the MA exam. My family congratulates me on the achievement. But once again, I am subject to the tyranny of obedience in the convent. Sr Claudia informs me that I have got third rank. How come, I wonder. Has someone played around with the marks after the final meeting in the university? Later, she explains: 'Memy, you can easily get a job as you have joined the convent. The second rank will be helpful to the other girl.' I know this is not fair, but I can hardly blame someone so senior of jealousy. My sole concern at present is to become a sister. I press for this even when Mother Provincial wants me to appear for a staff interview. 'Mother, why don't you let me become a sister first? How long have I been waiting for it!'

She reluctantly agrees. I continue my training. These are days of trials and punishments. I am being severely tested, as people think that I might become arrogant after my success in the postgraduate exam. I weep quietly in the Provincial chapel. My batch mates ask me: 'Why does the Mistress find fault with you always?'

'Because Jesus loves me intensely and purifies me through her,' I reply.

Some of the major punishments include removal from the job temporarily or permanently; denial of the right to vote or to be elected for a particular time; and dismissal from the local assembly for a certain period. But then, there are also minor punishments for sins like breaking or spoiling things, or for forgetting to put things back in their place after use. Sometimes this leads to comical situations. After gardening, a sister once left a pickaxe behind in the compound. Another time, someone misplaced a bucket. The two errant sisters had to kneel down in the refectory during the prayer before the meals, clutching the pickaxe and the bucket, respectively, while the sisters around them solemnly recited the verses. Imagine the silent mirth of the others at this amusing sight!

But there are other sisters who faced serious punishments. Sr Sudheena had to repeat her Postulancy, although it is a different matter that she herself was not confident of being fit to move up the next step, to the Novitiate. Due to some misunderstanding, she was harassed at the convent where she went for apostolic work, and this led to her Postulancy being extended as a punishment. Sr Kessy's Postulancy was prolonged by the authorities as she was hot-tempered. One of the authorities told me once that they wanted to send her away because of her irritable nature, but because she did all the menial work well, they thought of retaining her.

Six months after Postulancy, it is time for the Canonical Novitiate. The selection is done on the basis of an interview and evaluation by the Postulant Mistress. The period is one year and involves strict training. Only twice are we allowed to meet our parents in the parlour, that too for a limited period. We are not allowed to talk to any one except our batch mates, Novice Mistress, Mother Provincial and Councillors. This is the time when we attend serious classes on the Vows of Obedience, Chastity and Poverty, and on the theories about Community Life.

We have to write exams on various topics. The Sister (Novitiate Mistress) subjects us to many tests of character. Our every movement, word, action is scrutinized by the authorities. We have to endure many of their misunderstandings. A tension pervades the atmosphere, as we are constantly in fear of being sent away or kept back.

Once again, the staff interview comes up. This time I am forced by Mother Provincial to attend it. As I am selected, I am obliged to interrupt my preparation for the Canonical Novitiate and go back to Amala College as a teacher. Again, it is a stressful period for me, as weekends are spent in the Novitiate, and the other days with certain hostile sisters at Amala. I can never forget one misdemeanour by them when I had to submit again because of the Vow of Obedience. I joined as a teacher on 21 October and the Manager's order also confirms this date. But in the register there is a discrepancy—the date given there is 14 October, for no fault of mine. Perhaps it is an administrative oversight. The sad part is that I am compelled to sign in for a week, from the 14th to the 21st, when I was not in college but at the Novitiate. I obey but under protest.

My deepest regret is that I have started on this noble profession of teaching with false signatures. Woe to the Vow of Obedience in such contexts! After the four months of teaching, I return to the Novitiate, to re-join with a batch junior to me.

~

'Tea . . . tea . . . coffee . . . coffee . . .' O! I am still travelling. The second day has begun. The mobile shows missed calls from Sreejil, my nephew. 'Fr Joseph is desperate without your response. Please talk to him, sister mema.' Within an hour, the priest calls again. A message is sent to him: 'I am in Kerala. Details will be given to you after the 8th of September.' Repeated calls are ignored. Now one long day ahead.

2

THE WHITE LOTUS

I am still on the train. After their afternoon meal, people
around me are getting ready for a siesta. My interrupted
thoughts once again grow wings and fly to my Novitiate days.
In order to complete my Canonical Novitiate, I am to spend
almost five months with my junior batch. The sister-in-charge,
as indeed the whole convent, dislikes this batch. Among
the novices, some are prone to lying; a few have illicit
relationships with each other and so on. This enhances my
sufferings as well.

All my failures during those days are misinterpreted as
actions guided by the Devil. I know I have almost reached the
acme of my grief. Even my efforts at being a Good Samaritan
are misunderstood. Some mishaps occur too. Once I drop a
box of cassettes in the convent and all the plastic covers come
apart. On another occasion, while I am polishing the Bishop's
two crystal decanters, considered extremely sacred and precious,
because the wine for the Eucharist is kept in them, one slips

out of my hand and crashes on to the floor and is reduced to smithereens. Nothing worse can happen to anyone. I feel as if possessed by some terrible force.

Everyone who sees me, as lean as Gandhiji, passes unpleasant comments. Once when Amma comes on the day for visitors, I tell her with tears in my eyes: 'I would have come back home with my luggage, but for Jesus. Life here has become unbearable. But I stay on because He wants me to.'

As the period of my Novitiate is coming to a close, a Retreat is arranged for the senior and the junior novices. Once again, I am with my former batch. I am consumed by thoughts of the unique God experience I had in my previous stint as a Novitiate. A sister who prayed for me had two visions about my spiritual condition while I was still at Amala College. In one, there was a flood of light and all of us were walking towards Jesus, but I kept looking back every now and then. The second time, we were near a lake, when there was a flood of light. Everyone was spellbound by this splendrous sight, but I just went down to the lake and washed my face! It was upon this that one of the sisters, who guided me in spiritual life, had once commented: 'Memy, you are 99 per cent for Jesus. Whenever I pray for you, I have a vision that you lack one per cent of love for Him. Why don't you love Him 100 per cent?' I prayed hard and waited for an answer from Him. One day, I got an inspiration during the prayer. I told her: 'Sister, I see the vision of myself sitting in front of the altar at the Novitiate chapel. There I see Jesus leaping into my heart as in the case of the poet, Hopkins.' Gerard Manley Hopkins was taught to us by that very sister. He had both a spiritual and physical experience of Jesus, who suddenly captured his heart. The poet then converted and became a Catholic and later joined the monastery. The mortification he suffered for this was forsaking his poetry. In spite of great inner conflict, he gave up his God-given gift for the sake of a better religious life, as it was understood so. But when five sisters along with other passengers drowned in a shipwreck, the Rector wanted him to write a poem. 'The Wreck of the Deutschland', the well-known poem, was the outcome. He once again took up the pen in his 'praying hands' and mourned the death of the five petals or the five 'stigma' of the Crucified Jesus, representing the five nuns who had drowned. In the poem, he narrates his experience of the physical presence of Jesus, using the sprung rhythm, invented by him. I simply wonder why asceticism should demand that a man like him forsake his aesthetic sensibility, which helps one to revel in the joy of the God experience!

Although I wished for such a divine intervention from Jesus after re-entering the Novitiate, I have so far got only bitterness and negation. Anyhow, the days at the Retreat provide me some hope. The priest's sermons overflow with the Love of Jesus. Sparks of divine love are kindled in me. Being transported to a higher realm of spirituality, I relish the last days at the Novitiate. Nothing else binds me, other than His strong presence all around.

The day for Confession arrives. The place is abuzz with mysterious whisperings. I am the last person to know what has happened. People come and tell me, 'Memy, many of us are upset over a serious happening, especially Kusumam and Maria.' When I ask why, they continue, 'Don't you know, the priest has been kissing each of them when they have gone to him for an interview?' I remember him asking me permission to do the same, to which I refused. 'Why didn't these girls respond thus?' I ask myself. Is it fear or that Vow of Obedience ingrained in them? Now the whole atmosphere has been sullied. When the same priest sits in the confessional, nobody is willing to go to him. But after a while, someone comes and compels me to go for the Confession. After confessing my sins, I tell him: 'Father, I have something important to tell you. All the girls are disturbed because of one thing you have done. They are upset; and the whole impact of the Retreat has been spoilt. You should make amends immediately.' His argument is surprising. 'Molé, I have asked permission from each one of them. And only those who agreed, did I kiss. It is in the spirit of the Bible and Jesus.' He seeks to prove this to me with quotations from the Bible's Epistles, a little later. St Paul writes: 'Greet one another with a holy kiss.' (1Cor:16:20); 'Greet all the brethren with a holy kiss.' (1Thessa:5:26); St Peter says: 'Greet one another with the kiss of love.' (1Peter:5:14) Now he justifies his action by arguing that he means only 'holy kisses'. Anyway, he is angry and irritated. Soon after the Confession, is the Adoration-cum-Inner Healing ceremony, which is to be led by the same priest. Adoration is when Jesus is brought out into the exposed tabernacle. Inner Healing refers to the stages of our lives, from the womb to the present. He would like to meet me, the priest tells the Novitiate Mistress, who says he will have to wait until after the Adoration. When he comes for the ceremony, he is still upset. After the ceremony, I am taken to his room. All the others wait just outside as we are having a group prayer. Here is my chance to respond to his justifications from the Bible. 'Father, I think I understand what you are trying to prove. But with my limited intelligence, I know that the differences in culture matter. In the West, such physical expression of love is part of their culture. Among us, being warm-blooded, such conduct may be provocative in many ways.' Father suddenly turns rather gentle and concludes. 'If you had been a priest with the power of absolution, I would have confessed to you as a sacrament. Now I can only ask you to pray for me.' That is the end of that encounter. After the Retreat, he kneels at the centre of the chapel requesting the Novitiate Mistress and myself to lay our hands on his head and pray for him. He also suggests to her that if any novice still feels troubled, she should call me to lay my hands on her head and pray.

That night we are allowed to go to bed early, as we have been praying throughout, all these days. But something pulls me to the steps leading to the altar. Along with another novice, I kneel in front of the tabernacle. In no time, I lose myself. No movement, no sound, no light, no passing of time. I feel I am suspended in air. Suddenly, it happens—Jesus enters my heart. I feel the 'midriff astrain'—a physical experience of the Lord possessing the body. It seems my heart will burst; I feel transformed into a new being. Jesus is close to my heart and body. A constant presence! And my only desire is to be with Him. Heaven seems like Now and Here. Before every meal, we recite the prayer, 'Our Father', in the refectory; and this time, unlike others, I can sense His presence there. One of my batch mates asks: 'Jesme, I see you are in ecstasy when any prayer is recited. Can you share with us this great joy you experience?' All I can say to her is, 'This is the pure gift of Jesus. He will give it to every one of His brides. When we all experience it together, then it is Heaven on Earth.'

I have read the autobiography of St Theresa of Avila before, but didn't understand much of it. Now as I go through it again, I comprehend more than what is written there. Many parts of the Bible provide me new insights. I feel the same as the disciple Peter, who, falling down at Jesus' knees, after miraculously receiving the fish, tells him: 'Depart from me, for I am a sinful man, O Lord.' (Luke 5:8) During every Holy Mass, I am unable to bear His strong presence within; I fear my heart will soon break. And so I tell Him: 'Jesus, my Lord, depart from me. I can't hold you within me any longer.' With such pure joy within me, I can never think ill of anyone. When my Novitiate Mistress seeks my opinion about the novices in the junior batch, with whom I have stayed for more than four months, I cannot find anything to say against any of them. No jealousy, no pride, and no avarice exist for me these days. But later, I hear that three of the novices were sent away from the Novitiate due to some serious aberrations.

It is time for us to go to the Generalate—the highest authority of the Congregation—at Aluva for the common training. Fourteen of us are travelling there in a van. Throughout the journey, my friends ask me to lead the singing. But I can hardly wait for a break in all this to be with my Lord. I pray that I be left alone with Him, so as to have some quiet. But that very night, the Mistress at the Generalate announces that I have been selected for making the welcome speech at the inauguration the next day when the Bishops will be on the dais. I am surprised how these sisters know me. She reminds me, 'Haven't you come here to address the Superiors while you were in the Canonical Novitiate? The sisters here were waiting for you to come.' With His guidance, the welcome address goes off well.

A few of us have been selected by the authorities to present a full-length drama, of two hours, on Esther, a figure from the Old Testament. We spend almost a month training the actors, practising singing, making costumes, etc. Having a deep, husky voice, I have to sing for the male characters on stage, whose lip-movements are to be synchronized with my singing. It is strenuous training each actor for her role. Even those selected for the lead roles are stepping on to the stage for the first time. My friend and I are given the responsibility of polishing up the acting. When the great day arrives, we realize that a humorous item should also be put up during the recess, as the drama is serious and melancholic. I am chosen to do a mono-act. Directing the play and mono-acting is a strain on me. But with the Lord's grace, our efforts do not go in vain, as the audience comprising sisters from various Provinces, including the Principal from Amala College, appreciate the comic item and the drama.

We have classes on various subjects in Theology, taught by scholarly priests. Christology is taught well by a young priest who is about to go to Rome for further studies. Inspired by his classes, when we are allowed to use the library, I go straight to the Christology section and take out a book by Nikos Kazantzakis, called *The Last Temptation of Christ*. It is 1981, but none has so far ever spoken about this book. I ask Jesus to give me a sign if he does not want me to read it.

I reach up to the sixth chapter, where Jesus is nearing the brothel of Mary Magdalene. I find the poetic expression of the narrative as well as its central idea appealing. After all, it is only the greatest of people who recognize temptation and confront it, as Jesus did; most of us compromise because we do not even know when temptation comes. But I do not appreciate the notion of a wavering Jesus, because for me He is the one with strong convictions and faith, at all times. Despite reading in the book about Jesus' wavering, I doubt whether my strong faith in Him will ever be shaken.

Every day, I carry the book to the auditorium where we attend the classes. One day, the priest who teaches Christology begins the class with this question: 'Can anyone of you guess what the last temptation of Christ might be? I ask in the context of a book with the same title.' I am curious to know the answer, and to reply, so I quickly turn to the last pages of the book. My desperate movement is noticed by the priest, as all present, hundred novices and twenty-five junior sisters, stare at him. He comes down the pedestal and walks towards me: 'Let me see the book. From where did you get it?'

'From the library here.'

'How many libraries have I searched for this book? The librarian here also couldn't get it for me. Can you spare this book to me for a few days? I will return it before I go abroad.' I take this as the signal I had requested from the Lord—He doesn't want me to read this book, at least for now. By the time Father returns the book, my religious exams will begin and I would probably not get enough time to read it.

After the common training, we all come back to our own Provincialates, to prepare for our Vestition and the First Vows—to become 'white lotuses'. (Osho explains the term thus: 'White is the harmonious blending of all the colours, whereas lotus is the symbol of "sanyasam" as the flower rises above the pond but is in the pond—not of the world but being in the world.') During the years of my waiting for the Vestition (official ceremony after which you may wear the habit), there has been a change in the style of the 'habit' worn by the CMC sisters. When I came to join the convent in the year 1974, the sisters were wearing 'kapoose'—a white cloth stitched so that it covered the ears and the neck—which I liked very much. I did not know that it was a blind imitation of the attire worn by European sisters, who had to protect themselves from the severe winter. Even in our asceticism, we were influenced by European styles! In place of this habit, unsuitable for our hot weather, these days we wear one that leaves the ears and neck exposed.

Our parents come to the convent for suggestions to prepare for our 'wedding ceremony'—to know about printing invitations, the details of the tea party, etc. But we are not allowed to meet them. This becomes the hardest suffering for us to bear. On the eve of the most significant event in our lives, we are forbidden to meet those who gave birth to us. We will only see them in the church the next day. Anyhow, we accept all these sufferings in the true spirit, for the sake of the Lord whose brides we are about to become. The previous night we are all together, lying below the statue of Mother Mary in the hall. The eldest among us prepares us well for the 'total surrender'. Full of holy feelings and thoughts, we fall into the oblivion of sleep.

The auspicious day has dawned. All of us prepare for the ceremony, physically and spiritually. The event is in the same church where my brother's marriage took place. Except my chechie from Bangalore, all the family members attend. Fourteen of us wear white sarees, a crown made of white flowers and a white veil, that hangs from the crown, just like the bride dressed up for a wedding, and also a chain of ordinary white beads. We are taken to the church where the ceremony is arranged. We are seated on chairs in a room a little away from the church. Behind us stand our parents. Each novice is accompanied by her parents at the time of the procession, as she moves forward singing the song of total surrender. On reaching the steps leading to the altar, each one turns back, faces her parents, and removing the chain and veil, hands it over to them, in a gesture of farewell. It is a heartrending moment; parents often break down but the brides are supposed to suppress their sorrow. The parents bless us by laying their hands on our foreheads. Then leaving them, we climb up the stairs to the altar. The preparatory prayer is followed by the Mass. Each one publicly proclaims the Vows of Obedience, Chastity and Poverty over the mike and submits the paper recording our promises and which we have signed, to the Mother Provincial. After that we are given the habit, into which we change from our sarees, in an adjoining room. When we come back, we receive the chain with the CMC emblem, rosary, canonical prayer books, a lighted candle, a wreath of flowers for the hair, and so on, from the Bishop. Later, we kiss the ring of the Bishop as also the altar. The Mother Provincial, the Junior Mistress and some of the senior sisters climb the steps to the altar to embrace us. When the ceremony is over, we leave the church in a procession. The long-awaited spiritual marriage has occurred according to the norms of the Congregation and the society. I have become Jesme, 'Jesus and Me'. 'Without me you can do nothing,' says Jesus through the Evangelist John. (John 15:5b.) St Paul says this affirmatively, 'I can do all things in Him who strengthens me.' (Phili. 4:13.) Jesus should be before me. Then only can I exist.

Each family is given a room where they can have a tea party for their invitees to the ceremony. Next day, we are allowed to go home to celebrate with the family but should return by the evening. The family heartily congratulates me. My brothers remind me to seek a recommendation for them, whenever necessary, from their new brother-in-law!

The first night with Jesus as our bridegroom! We all go through a very solemn experience. We have a feeling of fullness, not unlike couples. Within a few days, we are ready, packing the necessities to set out on our apostolic work.

For five years after Vestition, we will remain junior sisters, wearing the white veil. We are under the surveillance of a Junior Mistress. The Mistress and the senior sisters evaluate our behaviour, conduct and manner, and based on that and the personal interview, we will be selected for the Final Profession.

We have a packed daily schedule. Before 5.30 in the morning, you should reach the chapel, and until 7.30, you have the Morning Prayer, Holy Mass and Novenas. After that, you spend fifteen minutes cleaning the house and surroundings. Until 9 o'clock, you have time for breakfast and personal work. And then you proceed to the field of work, to return maybe by 5.30 or 6 p.m. Then it is time for gardening or chapel duties. After bath, there is prayer in the chapel until 7.45 p.m., followed by supper and compulsory recreation. We sit around and chat or joke or complain, or read the circulars from the authorities. Then the long bell rings for the Great Silence. We go to the chapel for Night Prayer which lasts until 9.20 p.m.; those who haven't meditated for one hour, will do so until 10.20 p.m. Then, one has to spend half an hour in spiritual reading. This is the routine on an ordinary day.

For those of us, who are college teachers, it is only by 11 p.m. that one can prepare for the next day's classes. The other teachers in the college have no idea of this strict regimen, and want to push any extra work on to us, believing that we have a lot of free time. But our schedule in the convent is as hectic as theirs, with their family and teaching commitments. On feast days, or during Lent, we should spend more time for decorating the chapel or for prolonged prayers.

Penance is also to be performed. There is fasting on Fridays during Lent and before the feast days. During Lent and on some specified days, we give up eating meat. Working for half an hour extra and giving up one meal for the sake of helping someone in need are also means of penance. While doing penance, we should kneel down, our arms outstretched in prayer. During the training period, in the refectory during meals, one of us wears the crown of thorns on the head, carries the cross and walks up to the front and kneels. Every day, we recite Psalm 51, stretching out our arms, repenting for our sins, but on first Fridays, or every Friday during Lent, we scourge ourselves with a whip-like string, which we make ourselves, while reciting the psalm. It is a ritual meant to inspire awe. The chapel is dark, except for a candle on the altar; the sisters slowly begin to recite the psalm which resounds in the closed room, while we scourge ourselves of our sins with the whip. Earlier, we used to tie a barbed anklet-like object around our thigh or leg, under the skirt, for the sake of self-mortification. These days, we do not hear of this practice, though there is no dearth of other penances.

Before I entered the convent in the 1970s, there was a sort of class distinction even among the sisters. The less-educated and the less-privileged among the professed nuns belonged to a lower class, undergoing a different manner of training under a separate Mistress. These sisters, though also from the lower strata, were differentiated from the cheduthies as they, too, took the three Vows of Poverty, Chastity and Obedience, and wore the sister's habit. These nuns could not sit on chairs alongside other more privileged sisters but only on their 'trunks'. They were given jobs in the kitchen, parlour, fields or compounds. It was some consolation that by the time I came to join, the distinction between these two strata had been removed, at least to an extent. But it persisted in the minds of the sisters. There is a 'Fair Ethelamma' and a 'Dark Ethelamma' in the Province. The fair one belongs to the higher strata and the dark one to the lower, not only because of the difference in the complexion, but mainly because of the disparity in education and wealth. The two sections are treated differently.

I used to offer help to the dark Ethelamma in our convent, but was often dissuaded by the others, pointing out the distinction. Despite our proclaiming the ideas of justice and equality before God, such class distinctions exist in the convents and seminaries.

Two of us are allotted to St Maria's College Convent. I am transferred there from Amala College, to teach mainly the pre-degree students. My companion sister is always at the convent, preparing for the entrance exam to a course in Library Science which she is to join in Secunderabad. She becomes the pet of the Local Superior and also of all the other sisters in the convent, unlike me whose name the Superior doesn't even remember, and with whom the elderly sisters always find fault. But I am not bothered and tell her: 'I am almost in heaven in the college. What joy I get in teaching, you don't get. You enjoy here, whereas I enjoy things there. So it is balanced.' We are thick friends sharing every joy and sorrow, encouraging and consoling each other with prayer and support.

She and I are almost rivals in our love for Jesus. We vie with each other in our attempts to reach the chapel early in the morning to meditate and pray for longer hours, to kneel down for more than an hour at a time before Him, etc. Only such pious acts will fetch a 'good name' for us. Once, waiting outside the Bishop's room, she was reciting the rosary and I was reading a spiritual book. Seeing both of us, the Bishop remarked: 'The rosary in hand will edify the onlookers more than a book. She has done a better act of piety.' Kneeling down with folded hands is supposed to be the ideal expression of 'holiness'.

I am in the hub of things at college. The Principal considers me as her 'right hand'. I often have to supervise functions held in the college. She tells me: 'I have seen junior sisters who are humble; and some others who are intelligent. But I see in you both these qualities combined; keep it up.' The students and the teachers appreciate my way of teaching. The daily assembly prayer and other announcements are done by me.

The senior-most among us is Sr Maria, a very pious nun. When all the sisters and teachers in the college look towards me, I find this sister least concerned. Naturally, I am taken up with her as she is quite different from all the others, and I keep on trying to gain her attention. Within no time, she becomes my friend. It is a pure and sacred relationship. Neither of us can conceive of it as anything different. Her presence and guidance help me delve deeper into my bond with Jesus.

In convents, if two sisters are close to each other, the relationship is branded as 'special love'. Among us, this is supposed to be something sinful. Once, Bishop Kundukulam told the sisters, 'You all are very conscious about the special love between the sisters, as if that is the worst sin possible in the convents. But I warn you, beware of the long withstanding hatred among you. That is more detrimental.' So 'special love' is not as bad as hatred. Nevertheless, there are custodians assigned to observe and detect 'special love' between any pair of sisters. Once, such a watchful sister remarked to the Provincial, 'We can't say for sure there is "special love" between Sr Jesme and Sr Maria. But look around Sr Maria and you see Sr Jesme somewhere nearby.' Not that 'special love' is uncommon. But there is favouritism even in this case. When sisters who are influential develop 'special love', it is only murmured about in the community but never spoken of aloud. No punishment is meted out to them. But in the case of the junior sisters and the less important sisters, the fear of any relationship we share being viewed through the prism of 'special love', is always there. Hence, I am very cautious in dealing with Sr Maria; sometimes, we have to write letters to share urgent matters as we can't talk to each other in public; the 'watchdogs' may catch us unawares.

I am spared the blot of 'special love' but once, I find myself at the receiving end of someone's passion of a different kind. 'Sr Vimy' has been a senior sister-teacher in the Malayalam department and practically my colleague. Only gradually, I realize there is something odd about her. When we came to the convent, she had had a tiff with the Superior and other sisters, so I was asked to give speeches at functions in the convent, instead of her. She had been a rank holder and was very talented. To express her displeasure at this slight, she ignores me while showing favours to my batch mates, in my full view. I start making sincere attempts to gain her favour, never knowing that it will lead me into trouble. She has been caught having homosexual relations with a student in her hostel while she was the warden. The other hostellers themselves have seen things and reported them to their brothers and parents. At night, the boys passing on the road along the convent used to sing lines to her like: 'Sister, does the girl give you enough warmth; if not, shall we come to you?' The other sisters heard them, even if the sister concerned did not, as her room was a little away. Sr Vimy always created trouble in the convent. Not even the Mother Provincial could reprimand or punish her, as she used to shout at the authorities in front of everybody and create a scene. One day, after a severe quarrel, she was found missing; while searching for her, some even looked into the convent well, fearing the worst.

I did not know that the sister's 'girl' is attending my English classes. Whatever I say in class is echoed in the convent. I wonder how this is happening. Later, I realize that the girl is carrying news to her about me. Gradually, I find that Sr Vimy is 'after' me. She writes pages of 'love letters' and leaves them in my canonical prayer books. I shiver seeing these letters and always hand them over to my Mistress in the convent. She tears them off and throws them into the wastepaper basket. As I don't respond, Sr Vimy turns against me. Shouting at the hostellers who come searching for me, and throwing away the tape recorder when they bring it to be handed over to me, are some of her acts of revenge. The sisters realize that her anger is because of my spurning her advances. Indirectly, they hint that I should cooperate with her. I can't believe such things are happening, but as there is none to rescue me, I am forced to succumb to her attentions for a while. When all are asleep at night, she creeps into my bed and does indecent things to me which I hate but cannot combat. Our 'rooms' are a large hall divided up, and are separated only by sheets, so there are no doors which can be shut, to protect ourselves. She tells me that she is cautious to have sex only with women, lest she becomes pregnant. Referring to her former friend and sister, Sr Vimy wonders how she escapes pregnancy because occasionally she goes to the priests for sex. This is news to me. I can hardly swallow what she is saying. But I do wonder about her truth, considering my own plight to which everyone around wants me to turn a blind eye.

These days Sr Vimy is very peaceful and happy, talking to all, cracking jokes, and participating in the prayer programmes. The sisters are all thankful to me for restoring peace in the convent. They have guessed why Sr Vimy has become gentle, but no one is concerned about solving my problem. I carry on with a heavy heart and guilty conscience. At long last, a senior sister arranges for me to talk to a psychologist-priest who has come to preach in the college. After my sharing this traumatic experience, he explains to me: 'Out of a hundred people, five per cent tend to be homosexuals. The majority of them will end up in seminaries or convents as they don't like marriage. Their attraction towards the same sex leads them to such places.' Between tears, I tell him: 'I have been praying hard for her conversion, Father. This is difficult to endure. I never enjoy these things.' But, he says: 'Sister, you are praying for something impossible. Will you pray for the transformation of a girl into a boy? So impossible is your prayer for her to be otherwise.'

To escape from her clutches, without her knowledge, I go to the Mother Provincial and plead with her to either transfer her or me as I cannot endure this sort of life any longer. She mourns: 'There is no vacancy for you to be transferred to Amala College. She can be. But I don't dare to do so. She will never obey me and I will be humiliated in front of all the other sisters.' My response is a promise: 'You please put her name in the transfer order. The rest, leave it to me. I will persuade her to obey your order.'

I assure the Mother Provincial that I will do my level best to get this done. I believe Jesus will perform a miracle. I go to Bangalore to participate in a seminar. There a letter reaches me, announcing the transfer of Sr Vimy to Amala College Convent. I am only partly relieved as when I return to Thrissur, I will have to face her ire. I console her, saying there is no other way out but to obey, as we have vowed obedience. She rants at me: 'I will never go away from you. I don't believe in obedience at all.' I realize I have taken up a Herculean task and decide to wait for a miracle, through prayer and penance.

That day, the Mother Provincial has come to our college for some official matter. Through an attendant, Sr Vimy hands over a letter to her. I learn later from Sr Vimy that it is full of abuse and threat. How pitiable is the plight of the Provincial! The next day, I get a chance to meet the Provincial at the Provincial House. We talk about the transfer and return to the college in her car. But as soon as we get down, there is Sr Vimy who screams at the Provincial, forgetting my presence. Even the driver hears every word of hers: 'Are you a witch? How cruel and hard-hearted are you? How can the term "Amma" be used for you? What right do you have to transfer me? Don't you know I can't read much because of headache? Then how can I teach degree students?' I am dumbfounded, so are the Mother Provincial and those beside her. Still I hope against hope that Sr Vimy will leave for Amala College Convent.

It is the eve of transfer. The others who have got transfer orders are busy packing their luggage. But not this sister. By 10 a.m., I go to a building where she sits. Seeing me, she requests me politely: 'Will you please go to the chemistry laboratory and meet an attendant there? Tell her that I want some poison.' I cannot control my anger. The 'first explosion' in my life happens then. I can't believe it is me who is shouting: 'Don't you feel ashamed to say that you are a nun? Why can't you obey a transfer order from the authorities? Don't you trust God? Can't He help you there?' She is stumped by this unexpected outburst. Shivering, I continue: 'Don't come to me any more for anything. I really hate you.' I rush out of the building and hide in the convent. Till evening, she doesn't come out. I tremble, not knowing what is happening to her. But by 4 o'clock, she coolly comes out as if nothing has happened. Pouring milk into her glass, she tells the Local Superior: 'I haven't packed my things. Please send two junior sisters to assist me in packing.'

'Sr Vimy can call them,' says the Superior. She leaves me out, of course. Watching my friends helping her in packing, I joke: 'You two are fortunate for being selected,' to which Sr Vimy responds, quoting the Bible: 'Do not throw your pearls before swine, lest they trample them under foot.'(Mathew 7:6) Thank God, she has enough of a sense of humour to say this while leaving. Peaceful as a lamb, she gets into the vehicle and waves lovingly to me. Jesus has helped me to keep my word with the Mother Provincial. A queer chapter ends there for me. But what about other junior sisters who might have faced similar traumatic incidents? There are cases of sisters who still suffer in silence and fear.

Before her advances to me, Sr Vimy had a relationship with Sr Banny, who was working in a school. Once Sr Banny told me that it was Sr Vimy who took the initiative and trained her in these ways, though Sr Vimy had made it out to be the opposite. The first Principal of Amala College once shared with me the lesbian relationship of Sr Vimy with another sister in the convent. Following her transfer to Amala College, after her relationship with me, she had another student sister to 'play with'.

Then there was Sr Tressila, who as a second year novice, had a secret and wayward relationship with a senior sister. This continued even when she became a junior sister. When a rather young and beautiful sister came as the Superior of St Maria's Convent, many of the young sisters were 'after' her, but the sister closest to the Superior was Sr Tressila. The aged sisters had complained about the Superior's behaviour towards the young sisters, suggesting infatuation. After her tenure of three years, the Superior was transferred to the convent across the road from the college; from her room in the convent she could watch Sr Tressila in the college. She got permission from the new Superior who did not know anything about the relationship.

Later, a young and smart priest was made the chaplain of the college-convent. Every now and then, he was seen in that part of the college where Sr Tressila worked. Once, I even saw him pinching and caressing her in jest. Later, the relationship became a little more serious. Every day, she used to ring him up and narrate all that had happened in the convent. He would criticize those events during the next day's homily (a short sermon about the Bible passage assigned for that day). All wondered how he knew about those affairs. Only later we found out from the telephone records of the college that Sr Tressila's name was repeated daily against the phone number of the chaplain. Even the senior sisters noticed it. They complained to the Superior about this serious relationship, which led to a heated discussion in the convent. Sr Tressila was forced to confront the issue. I heard her shouting, in defence, that she had decided to elope with him soon and marry him. At this point, I intervened and entreated her to take leave for a few days and just go and pray and come back refreshed, which she did.

Sr Claudia had been the head of a department in Amala College when many of us used to pass comments on her special relationship with another sister called Sr Charisma. Many nights both of them were in the college with the justification that they had plenty of work to finish. Some of those nights, when I was in the college along with an attender to assist them, we would hear their giggles and other expressions of special love. Meanwhile, another sister started adoring Sr Claudia, leading to a rivalry between the newcomer and Sr Charisma. The former once shared with me the jealousy she had been enduring from Sr Charisma after Sr Claudia started expressing special love to her. I silently watch the trio as they move on.

Those are days when I come to know of certain violations of rules, but as a junior sister, I can only be a mute witness. Professional sisters, who have taken the Vow of Poverty like the other sisters, secretly take money and other valuables to their own families and relatives. These sisters are in charge of social service funds, and according to the rules, are not allowed to use them for helping their poor relatives. Sometimes, they take me along to their family homes where I see and hear things with my own eyes and ears.

Another matter I hear about relates to the irregularities in admission procedure in the college. According to government rules, the Scheduled Caste/Scheduled Tribe students are given a quota of a certain number of seats. To keep these seats for the management, sometimes false numbering is resorted to. Fictitious application numbers are allocated, whereby those seats can be grabbed. Once, the Principal and the assistants were gheraoed by the SFI activists for tampering with the seats of the reserved quota. These are occasions when my conscience pricks me, but out of fear I remain silent.

Petty politics also pervades the college. There is Subha, a feisty girl, who joins college and goes about the hostel propagating ideas about politics and the like, making some people think she is either a Naxalite or a Marxist. I am sceptical at first, but when I meet her personally, as the class representative, I find her to be sincere and open. Soon a 'hero' among the students, in her final year, she stands for election to the chairperson's post in the college union.

The teaching sisters and the Vice-Principal, who are against Subha, demand that I prevail on the Catholic students to vote against her. When I don't oblige, citing that teachers should not interfere directly in election matters, indirect methods are used. For all their machinations, Subha and her group win. When the results are announced, they are hooted by the degree students but are rescued from them by the others. I am proud of Subha who goes to her opponent with the first of the sweets she is distributing, offering her commiserations. That is the nobility in her; far more than in many of the elders.

That year continues to be a hard one for me. Whatever the College Union does, the blame falls on me. What follows is still sadder. The Vice-Principal finds a way to take vengeance. She gives the Principal names of those, including Subha, whose Conduct Certificates should be graded lower than 'Good'. Only on the day the certificates are to be distributed, do we tutors get to know. A teacher comes running to me shocked to see the lower grade of conduct, given to one of her best students. I too notice the same in many of the certificates in my class, which I distribute to my students with real grief. As I give Subha her certificate marked 'Not Satisfactory', she smiles at me, tears the paper and throws it into the wastepaper basket. Later, she repeats her pre-degree in a Sports College and comes out with flying colours. Two years later, at her interview for the degree course, when she is asked about her sports ability, she replies that 'whenever my mummy runs after me to beat me, I escape by running faster than her'. None at Amala College recognize her and she is selected to join the degree course in the sports quota.

Kshema's case gets me really agitated. She has devoted herself the whole year for special services to the college. When I learn that she is also given a Conduct Certificate marked with a lower grade, simply because she is not in the good books of the Vice-Principal, I go and meet the Principal. 'Sister, what wrong has Kshema done? If her parents ask any of the teachers, they will only eulogize her for all the good deeds she has done. Have you got any complaint against her?' The Principal can only say apologetically, 'Jesme, I never want these things to happen. I am under strong compulsion. If you can, will you please get back the certificate? I can give her a fresh one without the Vice-Principal's knowledge.'

The following day when I meet Kshema after the exam, she bursts into tears. 'Sister, what wrong did I do to you all? I couldn't do any of my exams well. My daddy and brother were about to rush to the Principal, but my mummy has prevented them, saying she will go to the college after my exams.' I try to console her and ask her to bring back the certificate the next day, on the promise that the Principal will issue her a fresh one. To my sorrow, I find the certificate in a deplorable condition. The clerk had already written 'Good' in all the certificates; the lower grade has been inscribed over this earlier remark. A fresh certificate is issued to Kshema. My regret is that I could save the future of only one girl by my intervention.

The time has come for our journey to the Generalate for the Juniorate course. Before that, people at the convent should record their opinions about each one of the batch, as a check on whether or not we should be granted permission for entering the Final Profession. There are four of us in the same batch: two are 'holy'; and the other two, including me, 'naughty'. When two of the so-called 'holy' sisters hear about the comments written by the senior sisters about them, they go on a non-cooperation strike in the convent, demanding that they be allowed to proceed to the Generalate. When I reach the Mother Provincial who reads out all the uncomplimentary comments about me, I remain cool. The criticisms seem to be lighter than what I had expected. Sarcastically, the Provincial says: 'When all write against you, a sister in the hostel kitchen is for you. She has written that you are a saint like St Theresa of Avila.' I feel so elated to know that at least that sister is with me. Besides her, my Junior Mistress has written well about me, though I never expected it from her. This gives me the passport to go for training for the Final Profession.

For eight months before the Final Profession, as part of the second year of Novitiate and Regency, we go to the Generalate for common training where we attend classes and write eleven exams altogether on various branches like Theology, Liturgy, Carmel Spirituality, Christology, Mariology, Spiritual Psychology, and the Bible, etc. Besides, we have plenty of manual work to do. We clean latrines, scrub drains, decorate the chapel, do gardening, till the ground and fetch cow urine from the shed, according to a weekly or daily rota. This is an occasion for me to prove my love to Jesus by aiming for the first rank in Theology. All my ranks so far are to be crowned by this one. I am very serious about my studies and classes. We are taught by Fr Vallooran, Fr Antony Narikulam, Fr Bosco Puthur, Fr Kanichai, etc. Despite the tough preparation, it is also a jovial time. I play the role of the Blessed Elias Kuriakose Chavara in a two-hour-long drama. To make me appear bald, a plastic paper smeared with a paste of flour is placed on my head. People fear that I may catch a cold as the paste remains on my head for quite a while. During the performance, I find our Mother General and the Provincials weeping, as they are reminded of the sufferings of the Blessed Chavara. The next day, the Mother General says: 'Jesme, I found you to be just like our Founder. If only you become like him in real life!'

The Theology exam results are put on the notice board, and to my great joy, I find I've got the first rank. Raising my heart to Jesus, I say: 'You are a Wonder, Lord!'

After the course, begins the spiritual training—meditation,

Retreats and Monthly Recollection—for our Final Profession. By the middle of May, we return to our own Provinces and prepare for the ceremony. In the public function, we are committed perpetually to the Lord. Ceremonially, we are given the black belt, the symbol of the Final Profession. Now on, we are considered as 'Senior Sisters', without a Junior Mistress to guide as well as scold us. Once again, I come back to St Maria's College to resume my work as a teacher.

3

THE CELESTIAL THISTLES*

Life as senior sister gets off to a good start. I look forward to teaching and deepening my spiritual development. But little do I know of the thistles that will be strewn on my path. Even before I have quite settled down, I am asked to appear for the selection test for M.Phil. course in the University of Calicut. For the five merit seats, out of the batch of six, more than hundred candidates come for the entrance test followed by an interview. To my surprise, I am at the top of the list. Having taught only General English to pre-degree students for all these years, I have to struggle to come up to the level of the four other teachers, who have been teaching degree and postgraduate students. One of them has taught postgraduate students for twenty-two years and another candidate has only a year to go for retirement. During the ten days' Onam holidays, I stay in the hostel to do some reading. Very soon, I

---

*(2 Corinthians 12:1–10)

find myself catching up with the others. We are a lively bunch. Once a colleague puts up a poster on the board behind our professor, which reads, 'Never trust a smiling teacher.' Another time, our teacher colleague sends us by post a photo with the caption, 'Our Group Photo'. Opening the envelope, we find a cartoon of six skeletons standing in a row—talk about overworked and starving research students!

In the first semester, we have course work and exams, but when the second semester starts, we are required to select an author and a topic for our research. My favourite poet is Robert Frost, but the head of the department believes it is not a good idea. Sarcastically, he says in class once, 'Someone is going to work on Frost, I hear. What is more to do on Frost, I wonder!' All look at me. When I persist: 'Sir, can't I work on something new on Frost?' he says, 'Oh! Of course, you can, sister. But each time you try to write, you will remember what I have said.' Upset, I guilelessly ask, 'Are you cursing me, sir?'

'Who am I to curse you, sister? I am telling you the fact.' There ends our discussion.

When I tell my classmates about the new approach I am going to use to analyse Frost, they are all impressed. New Criticism is the latest tool in literary theory then and using it, I seek to explore 'The Parabolic Pattern in the Poetry of Robert Frost' for my thesis. My research not only investigates the pattern but also compares and contrasts many of his poems with the Parables of Jesus. Cleanth Brooks and New Critics argue that paradox is the crux of poetry, even of the Romantic Poets. In my thesis, I argue that this paradox is present even in prose writings, including the parables. Citing Frost's interest in the paradoxical use of language in the parables, I provide a new definition for them. I start by showing that Frost's poems are all parables as well as paradoxical, and end by comparing ten poems of Frost with the Parables of Jesus in the Bible.

But without the permission of the head of the department, how can I work on this proposal? In His own mysterious way, Jesus comes to my rescue. My Appan is admitted to hospital. He is found to be suffering from advanced cancer of the oesophagus, and it is too late for any treatment. My department head's wife, too, is diagnosed with cancer. When we meet, we discuss about the condition of the two patients. On the day of our project scrutiny and selection, he comes to the meeting but is suddenly called to his wife's side. He delegates the responsibility to the next professor in seniority. This professor is much impressed by my discussion and in no time shows the green flag.

The last time I saw my Appan, was when I went to seek his blessings for my second semester exams. After the exams are over, I am eager to go over and tell him about them in detail, as he is always curious to know. The last time I asked permission to go home, the Local Superior had scolded me for visiting him often. She had warned me not to ask for leave for a long time. I hesitate to ask again. The next morning Appan leaves us all forever. I can now only weep near his dead body, regretting my ill luck. That night, I cannot remain beside him, as the rule is that we should not stay overnight at home—now this has changed. I reach the convent around 6 p.m., before the gate is closed, feeling cruelly separated from my father's presence even at this time. My request to sit in the chapel after Night

Prayer is rejected by the Provincial, Mother Claudia, who is there on an official visit. The next morning even after Mass, I am told to stay in the convent on the grounds that the aged sisters there were not allowed to attend their fathers' funerals, as that was the rule in those days. The funeral is at 9 a.m.; I am allowed to reach home only by 8.45 a.m. After everything is over, I come back to the loneliness of my suffering.

For several months thereafter, I cannot reconcile myself to Appan's passing away. Every time I pass by Amala Hospital where he was taken, I break down. I couldn't stay at home to share my grief with the family and find solace. Some sisters recognize my grief but I am unable to share it with them. They will not understand my affection for Appan's many qualities; for them, he was not a good family man.

I immerse myself in study. In the university, the professors in the department select the scholars whom they will guide for the dissertation. None of us wants Prof. R.V. as we have heard that he is a perfectionist and makes students keep rewriting their work until it is perfect. My only prayer is not to get that professor as my guide, as once we have completed one year and are back to teaching, I won't get that much time for research and will not be able to manage with someone like him. When the official letter comes, my name has been put against Prof. R.V.'s! An interview with him follows and then we all go to the American Studies Research Centre library at Hyderabad for material collection. When I submit my dissertation, I realize that Jesus blessed me with the best supervisor possible.

A letter comes, congratulating me for getting the first rank in the M.Phil. course. At a get-together to felicitate Bishop

Kundukulam on the Festal Celebration at the Provincialate, I meet the Provincial, Mother Claudia, and share this good news. Instead of being pleased, she is angry, and asks, how come? According to the professors she has asked, a teacher with twenty years of postgraduate teaching experience is the best scholar there. As an excuse, I have to tell her that my dissertation and viva-voce fetched higher marks than hers. I am grateful to my Jesus for taking care. Little do I know that as the Provincial, it is just the first of my troubles with her.

Being the class tutor, I try to inculcate some social consciousness in my students. I help make them aware of the less-privileged students in their own class. The rich are exhorted to love and care for the poorer sections and to render them financial help in times of need, without belittling them. By the time they finish college, they have developed a consciousness for acts of charity.

Two of the teaching sisters are sent for M. Phil. that year and I am entrusted with the extra-curricular activities of which they were in charge. The Principal, Sr Gladita, appoints me as the 'overall in-charge'. Whenever some duty comes, I am called from my class. I decide never to say 'no' to the Principal, as two sisters are away from the college, and she is known to lose her temper, to the point of flinging files. There have been Principals who used to shout even before. The only way to deal with them is to adjust as much as possible.

Being the 'overall in-charge', I soon realize is a double-edged sword. An NSS camp is to be held and the NSS officer insists on my assisting her. I am brought to the Principal's room, where the Vice-Principal and the NSS teacher, besides the

Principal, are present. When asked, I demur, saying, 'Sister, you know all the work given to me in the college and in the convent. Still, do you want me to assist her?' But then, remembering my resolve not to refuse, I oblige. But only later I come to know of their duplicity—they wanted me to refuse so that I could be blamed; the staff would then turn against me.

I keep getting tossed between the Principal and the Local Superior, in preparing for this camp, usually conducted during the Onam holidays. At every stage, I invite the Principal to discuss the details, to get her permission for travel and the like. I take her excuses to evade me as genuine. When I have to go out for printing the notice-cum-invitation, the Local Superior intervenes. 'The classes are over by 3.30. You should reach the convent soon after.' Shocked, I ask her: 'When shall I do my "overall" work, in that case? Let us wait till the Principal comes from the college.' My hopes at that time are pinned on Sr Gladita. She will clarify everything to the Superior. When she comes, I rush to her, but she too gives me an unexpected reply: 'First of all, you are a nun in the convent. So obey the Superior.' Amazed, I blink at her: 'Sister, then how can I perform my duties in the college?' Another astounding response: 'You write down on a piece of paper what all work you can do from 9.30 a.m. to 3.30 p.m.' I have caught on by then that they are playing a game which they have already rehearsed. I hastily go to the chapel and ask Jesus for succour. On a piece of paper, I jot down: 'With understanding and freedom, I can do all the work entrusted to me.' On reading this, the Principal delivers the final blow. 'You can take leave for as long as you want, take rest, sleep or relax. After that, we will decide what all to do.'

I take this in a positive spirit and console myself. Next day, I remember that I had kept in the TV shelf, two VCDs, which belong to my brother in Damam, and should be returned to him. I search for the TV key in the usual place but find it missing. The electrician tells me that the key has been removed and kept elsewhere, with instructions not to give it to me. From that day, I vow not to touch the TV.

From the Constitution of the Congregation, I read that one sort of punishment for a sister is to set her apart from all work. Now the picture is becoming clearer. Another mode of punishment used on me is that all the sisters, especially the student sisters who I teach, are asked to avoid any contact with me. Once I request a sister to fetch me the bottle of Vicks placed on my table. She brings it to me out of love and respect, when immediately she is summoned to the Principal's room. When I see her come out trembling, I grow suspicious. Only then do I come to know of the authorities' attempt to ostracize me.

Other sisters, too, suffer like me. Sr Sajeena is thoughtful and sometimes questions the state of affairs, unlike the others. She is also humiliated by the Provincial in many ways. After three years as juniors, the sisters are blessed with black veils. It is a small but solemn ceremony, marking their preparedness for becoming senior sisters. Even as the sisters reach the chapel, the veil for Sajeena is removed from the pile placed on the altar for blessing, and she is asked to step back. She swoons as she has been sundered from her batch mates. Her isolation continues even as a senior sister. When she eventually becomes headmistress of a convent school, the Provincial has her removed from the post. It is only much later, when Mother Claudia is elected as General Councillor at the Generalate, on returning to Kerala after her assignment in Delhi, that we heave a sigh of relief as she will never be re-elected as our Mother Provincial. But until then, we had to suffer for six long years.

New kinds of punishments are in store for me. One day, the Provincial tells me that she has been waiting for some sort of physical ailments to afflict me so that I can be taken to the hospital, but I am as healthy as ever! I respond with much satisfaction: 'Jesus will never let me off from my duties.' All of a sudden, she retorts: 'If there is no physical illness, I will have to take you to a psychiatrist for treatment.' This is beyond endurance. Somehow, I approach the Principal and tell her that the Provincial is planning to take me for mental treatment. Tearfully, she pleads with me not to go with her. 'But, Sister, won't that be disobedience on my part?'

'No, Jesme. If you are punished for not obeying, put the blame on me.' I sense that she has a soft corner for me. Jesus has transformed one of the wolves into a lamb.

What has prompted the authorities to attempt mental treatment on me? I start ruminating. Maybe they never appreciated my desire for freedom and the ways and means I adopted to achieve it. Moreover, they could not digest my mixing of spirituality and aesthetics in order to reach God. My frankness and straightforwardness may lead to many of their secrets being revealed, they feared. My questioning of many of their decisions and practices may have reaped for me the displeasure of the authorities. Perhaps that is why they want to curb me, to break me and silence me.

Meanwhile, Amma visits me in the parlour. Between tears, I explain everything to her. She consoles me as best as she can and requests me to endure all this for the sake of the Lord. But then, things reach a climax. At night, the Superior announces that the Provincial has been in the college parlour waiting for me. The watchman leads me across the road to the college. Reaching there, I meet an attender girl staring at me, terrified. She warns me about a man with a moustache sitting inside. 'Sister, please pray well before you enter.' I, too, am shocked; at 8.30 in the evening, I don't expect to see a man inside the college. As I enter, I see both the Provincial and this man. He starts questioning me about my mental condition. Reluctant to answer him, I turn to Mother Claudia and plead with her to understand. She compels me to cooperate with the doctor. I refuse and once again beg the Provincial to let me be. 'Mother, have mercy on me. Just ask Jesus whether to punish me or not. I don't think He will agree with your deeds.' She insists that the Congregation is doing me a favour by spending money on my mental treatment. I should be thankful to authorities like her. I press, 'Mother, I am quite normal. Please understand me. It is getting dark. Allow me to go to the convent.' Without waiting for her consent, I run outside. The watchman sitting there has been given instructions that when I come out, I am to be taken to the convent. Immediately, he leads me through the road to the convent. Racing to my room, I throw myself on the cot and start weeping: 'Jesus, tell me, have I turned mad? Is it just that I don't realize it?' I now see the bleeding face of Jesus looking at me in utmost mercy and uttering: 'See my agony. You are partaking in my suffering.' What solace this is to me! Will the Provincial come after me right now for further punishments? I fear the arrival of the Provincial every second for further punishments, but then slowly slip into sleep. Next morning, the sister from the kitchen tells me that she has been kneeling the previous night and praying for me with outstretched arms.

A prayer service is now held in the convent for my 'recovery'. My batch mate, Sr Jeevan's pitiful weeping breaks the silence and solemn air in the chapel, as she cannot bear the treatment being meted out to me. Sr Maria resolves to skip a meal for forty days, to pray for my sake. Later, she tells me, 'Sister, you are not meant to be confined as an ordinary nun in a convent, but to be someone greater.' She advises me not to reply to the authorities, and hence I put a stone in my pocket as a reminder to keep my mouth shut! As no one is allowed to speak to me, often we have to converse in writing.

That evening, Amma calls me. 'Memy, a very important thing I have to tell you. If ever you are forced to go to the mental hospital, don't go. Tell them that your mother is alive. Only your Appan is gone. I will file a case against them.' I burst out crying; between sobs, I describe the happenings of the previous night and how I escaped. Then she reveals, 'Molé, I came there the other day just to watch you and see whether you are insane. A sister phoned and told me to take you to a psychiatrist. I wanted to hear from yourself the details of what is happening. Seeing you quite normal, I didn't tell you anything.'

'Amma, why didn't you give me a warning?'

'I never thought they would really do anything.'

Mother Claudia calls the next day. I am at Amala College, as one of the three judges for the Poets'/Artists' Day. It is held in honour of Sr Mary Leo, and prizes are awarded to the best presenter of a poet and artist. My attendance is proof of my sanity, of my sensibility and rationality being intact. So my pleading to leave me alone for some days at least, finds a positive response. And the ordeal is over for now. But not for long.

As Sr Gladita, Principal, has permitted me to register for Ph.D, I go to meet my M.Phil. supervisor, Prof. R.V. Before going, I ask her whether to get permission from Mother Claudia, the Provincial. She clarifies that as laid down in the rules, she as Principal has already given permission to send sisters for research. I decide to go in and at least say a 'hello' to him. The professor says that he has no slot at the moment but that he will accept me soon after the poet Sacchidanandan submits his thesis. 'Let us begin our first discussion today itself, sister. Why can't you start reading some authors? If you are interested, you can work on Edward Taylor.' This is followed by three more discussions with Prof. R.V.

Meanwhile, I see Mother Claudia and talk to her about the author on whom I am working. She is much impressed as she is familiar with Taylor's writings and we talk for a while about them. But soon, all this is forgotten and she turns against me again. She accuses me of not informing her about my Ph.D plans. I clarify, 'Mother, I asked the Principal whether to inform you, to which she replied that you have already given us permission. Moreover, I came to you and talked about the author. Mother, don't you remember my reference to Edward Taylor and then your remark that he is a pastor-poet?' Thank God! Now she remembers. But despite this, she continues to rail: 'You haven't got permission from the Council.' I have never heard of this so far. Many sisters have gone for research. To the best of my knowledge, they haven't waited for such permissions. But, Mother Provincial is undeterred. She asks me to go to Prof. R.V. and withdraw my research proposal. She uses the issue to pull me up for missing the prayer days. The big blow follows. When I tell her, 'Mother, how many times have I asked the Principal for leave in order to go for prayer?' she retorts, 'This time you will be granted leave. Request for one and a half years' leave on Loss of Pay.'

'I don't need that much time for prayer. Just give me leave for one month, Mother,' I plead. She insists, 'No, Jesme. Obey me and request for a long leave. Then only we can appoint a new staff.' Without any further objection, I agree and sign the leave application. The Principal, who is less hard-hearted, breaks down, and I console her saying it is good for all that I pray longer.

When Mother Claudia comes for the Provincial visit, an official inspection by the authorities of each convent, she wants me to go personally to the Principal and the Superior to ask pardon for all the restlessness I have caused them. I do it most sincerely. Then I am ordered to stand up when the community assembles for the concluding meeting and asked to seek pardon from all the sisters. In the most humble way, I obey that too. When I plead for pardon, I notice many of the sisters are weeping.

Before going, I meet my supervisor and tell him that I am leaving for one and a half years; he can give the chance offered to me to a more fortunate candidate. He is upset and wants me to keep the candidature pending. I demur, 'Sir, I am going to become an ascetic. Hence, I don't need the degree.' He tells me that perhaps Sr Claudia wants to guide me—she had mentioned this to him once, it seems. I tell him, 'No, Sir, if ever I do research, it won't be under her.' He asks me, 'Why is she always against you? Whenever a reference comes up, she bears down heavily against you, despite my praise.' All I can say is, 'I don't understand the reason, Sir.' Thus, I bid him farewell.

More composed, I proceed to a prayer centre named 'Tabor' at Palai. I enjoy each day there, even though the sister-in-charge is asked to watch each of my movements. She even hides the letter sent to me by two sisters of St Maria's College. Later, a junior sister, while helping to arrange the in-charge's trunk, sees it and informs me about it. How will they justify all this, I do not know!

At some point, a sister from Daya College reminds the Principal that I cannot go on a 'long leave' as I have a bond of one year of continuous service in the college for having done M.Phil. under the Faculty Improvement Programme (FIP). After a few months of prayer, I am therefore asked to rejoin. Coming back, I live quietly. As a very dutiful sister, I close my eyes to the Principal's misuse of the college funds, as also remain silent about her 'special love' towards an attender girl and the librarian sister who is also the bursar of the college.

A Superior, who understands my point of view, has come to the convent. I don't receive any favours from her, instead there are many restrictions, but I accept it as I respect her holiness. Amma's sixtieth birthday comes and all her children want to invite her to their homes to celebrate. But she has another plan: 'I like to celebrate my sixtieth birthday at my nun-daughter's place. We all will join the Mass there and serve the sisters breakfast. Then with their blessings, I will cut the cake.' Everyone is agreeable. On the eve of her birthday, she meets the Superior and requests for permission; but it is refused. All are upset. At this last moment, what is to be done? Amma makes a quick adjustment. 'Let us all attend the mass at Dolour's Church. We shall ask the sacristan to show a place to cut the cake. Then I will go to a prayer centre and pray the whole day.' Those days, sisters are not allowed to attend the Mass in the parish church. Fortunately, I get permission to attend the Mass with Amma. It is pitiable when she has to plead with the sacristan for a place to cut the birthday cake. Later, when a sister's parents' wedding anniversary is allowed to be celebrated in the convent followed by dinner at the refectory, in the enclosure, I remember the plight of Amma on her sixtieth birthday.

When the authorities display 'double standards' or duplicity in their judgements and manner of punishments, I wonder at the practice of 'justice' here. A sister undergoes a hysterectomy operation and stays in the sick room for rest. I am puzzled at the remark of the Superior, that she is relieved that the sister's uterus has been removed, or else when she spends her nights elsewhere, they are all scared. And she speaks of the time when this sister was caught red-handed by the public from the room of a priest at night. As she was influential with the authorities both in the Province and the Bishop's House, she escaped unscathed. This incident is confirmed by many within the convent and outside. It also appeared in three paragraphs in a popular crime magazine, a yellow journal, but the Superiors ignored all of it, whereas some of the less influential sisters are punished for even silly acts of disobedience or doubts about their chastity.

Our practice of the Vow of Poverty is rather queer, incomprehensible to the people outside. The huge amount of our college salaries and any other income we get is transferred to the Mother House, the Provincialate, for central pooling. 'From each according to their capacity and to each according to their need' is the norm practised in the Congregation. The late Bishop Mankuzhikary once told the public: 'You want to meet the real Marxists. Look there!' And he pointed at the priests and the sisters. Each sister is entitled to a 'per head'— an amount of around Rs 300 or so. The amount is collected by the convent treasurer. Only a percentage of it can be spent for food items. Every month, the treasurer along with the Superior grumbles that the expenditure is excessive. A discussion to reduce some of the necessities follows. We are to forsake food in the evening, or have coffee without milk, or give up fish or meat for long periods. We feel sad every day when we enter the refectory—the dining room—as we are reminded about this discussion.

Once the Superior moaned that the money to buy firewood had been used up for other items, and that she had no solution for it. Somehow, I used my influence to grab the chance of evaluating answer scripts at the university for a month and was able to provide the Superior with enough money. All the feasts are preceded by fasting, but the people outside are only aware of the feasting. Still, the poverty endured by the poor is indeed graver than what we experience in the convents.

The professed sisters get all their necessities from the convent. We are blessed to be free of any worries in the world. As safe as in 'Noah's Ark', we live more secure than the richest Ambani or Bill Gates. We do not have to experience any worry over money of the kind that upsets a patient undergoing expensive treatment. Once a preacher remarked: 'The Ascetic and the Rich are synonymous terms nowadays.' But there is an arrangement of 'pocket money' in some of our Provinces, in order to teach us the value of certain items and to know how to handle money faithfully. The amount began with Rs 25 and has now been raised to Rs 75 per month. At the end of the year, the balance amount is to be handed over to the Superior. Expenses for personal travel, postage, phone calls, slippers, umbrella, soap–paste–brush, etc. are all to be met from this pocket money. The details of the expenditure should be jotted down in a book and every month, it has to be verified and signed by the Superior. There have been times when I used to weep for lack of money to buy slippers. One time a sister, a staff at the office, whispered in my ear: 'Don't keep on moaning. Learn to make adjustments in the other financial accounts of the convent. That is how we all survive.' I don't have other accounts and hence I solve the problem by asking my brother or sister or first cousin to buy me slippers or an umbrella.

But I envy the Diocesan priests whose case is quite the

opposite. These priests have the right to own private property whereas the priests belonging to the Congregation have the Vow of Poverty; but even they have more liberty in handling finances than the nuns.

In our Congregation, we rarely have a separate house for aged sisters. Our preference is to retain the aged or sick sisters in the same convents so that they will get ample attention. Besides, the younger sisters get to learn how to look after those who go through old age. An aged sister, Jainamma, at Amala Convent, deserves special mention. Belonging to a prestigious family, she unconsciously prefers sisters of high-class families to those of the lower classes. Towards the latter days of her life, she has lost her normal senses, to a certain extent. But other than some aberrations, she is a very sweet granny. However her unusual traits are hard to endure. There are times when she takes a coconut, keeps it on her shoulder, and balancing it with one hand, walks outside the compound along the road. She is brought back to the convent by those who know her. Occasionally, her mental imbalance prompts her to collect her excreta in a mug and hide it under the cot in her room. The foul smell leads us to the hidden place. When she sees a sister who works in the kitchen, she orders her to clean it. But when I try to take the mug, she prevents me from doing it as she knows about my background and degrees. But if I forcefully take it, she assists me in the attempt. Whenever she is found missing, you can see her in my room lying on my cot and sleeping. We all are competing in looking after her in that state of oblivion and helplessness. Finally, she is admitted in a nursing home, falls down from the cot, gets into a coma, is brought back to the convent, and dies peacefully, getting care from each one of us.

Our Vincentamma is another innocent nun with old-age problems. She is naughty but very caring. When she loses her senses, she spreads her excreta on the walls near her. When we go to meet her, she holds us with her soiled hands. But still we all love her and compete in serving her. There are nuns in their old age who go to the altar with a bottle of eye drops, asking Jesus to pour it into their eyes. A retired Principal who becomes blind in her old age has an uncontrollable fascination towards the chaplain. Many of the goody-goody, holy nuns in their old age develop an infatuation towards chaplains. All their suppressed emotions explode in their old age as they lose their self-control. The priests also respond to them a little, so that they are not frustrated. It is a consolation that the sisters in their old age are well cared for in the convents. One cannot expect this much attention and caring even in one's own family.

But, in the case of the aged priests, the problem is the other way around. They are attended by male servants who are very careless in their job. A priest-uncle, one of my mother's relations, scalded himself, pathetically falling into the hot water pot kept in his bathroom. The servant had gone off after keeping the water, and uncle could get help only very late as nobody was nearby. There are numerous incidents of such negligence in these places.

All the aged nuns are given some duties to perform so that they don't feel useless at any time. But the majority spend most of their hours either in the chapel or in their rooms, doing silly jobs. I used to wonder why we don't make them available to those outside. Very few of them go for house visits. My suggestion to the aged nuns is to spend a part of their time with the students in the college or the school and just listen to them; if possible, share their experiences with the youth. Their participation in social activities will heal them and society.

But even in darkness, there are wisps of light. The news of the General Councillor's death by accident leaves me in deep sorrow. She had concern and understanding for me. I want to attend her funeral, and am waiting for a chance to go, when I get a phone call from the Provincial, Mother Claudia, to meet her urgently: 'Jesme, I am going to attend the funeral of the Councillor. Tonight, you stay in the Provincialate with the composer Sr Pelerine and discuss about some songs to be recorded.' Though disappointed, I cannot disobey the order. Mother has placed her full trust in me. I spend the whole night working with Sr Pelerine who is a very saintly sister, flowing with the love of Jesus. She teaches me her constant prayer: 'Jesus, empower me with your masculine [enormous] strength and love.' If anyone is to be canonized from our Congregation, I would suggest Sr Pelerine's name. Next day, we go to Fr Paul who is an ardent admirer of the sister's compositions as well as a good music composer himself. Handing over the songs to him, we make necessary arrangements for a studio, to produce an audio cassette of songs on Mother Euphrasia.

Born in 1877, she had joined CMC and spent her life at the convent in Ollur, Thrissur. From the very beginning, she had been leading a life of penance, mortification and self denial. Later, she began to have visions of Jesus, Mother Mary, and many other saints. Her life of piety and virtue attracted many people towards her, to request favours from God through her. Even after her death in 1952, many received blessings, healing and many other gifts by her intercession. Now she is proclaimed to be one of the Blessed by the Pope.

These are days of spiritual aridity in my life. My friend Sr Maria, who is a spiritual guide to me, compels me to spend an additional hour at prayer in the college prayer hall. 'I feel so dry inside that I cannot pray, sister.'

'Sit there, just looking at Jesus. That will cure your aridity,' she advises. I obey blindly and gaze at Jesus hanging from the cross; 'who are you?' and 'who am I?' are my constant questions. After an hour, I come away, hoping that some day He will touch me. And this happens in an extraordinary way.

With much difficulty, I reserve the recording studio for three dates. Sri Murali is entrusted with orchestration and Sri Santhosh Babu is the lead male singer. Within four days, all are ready for recording under the direction of Fr Paul. I am in charge of all the arrangements. My family being close by is helpful. The artists are put up at my younger sister's place, while she shifts with her family to another house. All of this is done out of gratitude to the late Mother Euphrasia, the would-be saint.

The recording begins; the cassette is called 'Sannidhi'. Among the artists from Ernakulam is a known figure named Govind. Due to his negligence, much time is wasted. When he comes out of the recording room, I tell him off and exhort him to be more careful next time. He takes it lightly and asks my name. Then he plays with it and I explain: 'Jesme. That is coined from Jesus and me.'

'Will you replace Jesus with my name?' he jokes with me. I am shivering all over; pointing at him, I declare: 'Don't play with Jesus or me. It is like playing with fire.' He laughs aloud and casually continues chatting with a sister standing near me. After that I find Govind always behind me. He wants additional 'pappadams' from me; when he has headache, he wants medicine from me; when it rains and I am in the ground with an umbrella, he runs towards me in the rain and shares my umbrella. He tells me that after years of search, he has found his soul-mate! 'When did your "sickness" begin?' I ask him. 'The moment I saw you,' he replies. I just laugh it off as a joke. That night, we are busy in the studio until early dawn. Then some of us go to the convent of the late Mother Euphrasia for a few hours' rest. After Mass, we are to get back to the studio. While lying on the bed, I have a flashback of that day's events, especially the caring behaviour of Govind's. With a smile of happiness, I look at the tiny cross hanging in the room. 'Jesus, who is Govind compared to you? You are the most handsome man I know—the wealthiest, the smartest, the wisest and the most sincere and caring.' Within the twinkle of an eye, a stream of love wells up within me from nowhere, and I experience the joy of being His bride again. It is an ecstasy that is both physical and spiritual, different from all my former experiences. I realize that through Mother Euphrasia and with Govind as an agent, Jesus has broken my granite-like soul, and made me the channel of His Love, Peace and Joy. As He touches me, my spiritual aridity has given place to ecstasy. And I believe this is the gift of Euphrasiamma who is indeed a saint!

Very soon, I am brought back to earth. The inauguration of

As Faustus, in the last scene of my (degree) college production of Marlowe's play, *Dr Faustus*. Won prize for best actor in the Calicut university inter-zonal competition.

In fancy dress, as a pujari, at a college festival.

Procession during the Vestition ceremony

As a Junior Sister

Blessings from the Bishop
during the Vestition
ceremony

With my Novice Mistress
who prepared me for the
Vestition

With my three sisters, after the Final Profession

On a college trip to
Ooty

Singing merrily in
the bus during a
college trip, with
other teachers

During a college trip

With my entire family, after the Final Profession

the Golden Jubilee of the college takes place under a new Principal, Sr Susie. Plans are being discussed for the year-long celebrations. The foremost suggestion is to get donations during admissions. All of us are proud of our college never demanding donations for admissions or appointments. So when the topic comes up for discussion, I object to the idea. 'For forty-nine years, we managed without donations. Why do we have to spoil our name and policy in this auspicious year?' I am the only person to protest against taking donations. At the next meeting of the teaching staff, I sit in a corner with bowed head, but keenly watch their reactions. Many of the staff members are for the proposal: 'Get as much money as possible, sister. Let us benefit from the "wealth-sacks" in and outside the town.'

I sense a jovial mood about me. The Principal, who is uneasy about my presence there, is eyeing every movement of mine. A decision is taken in favour of accepting donations. Next day, I am abruptly summoned to the Principal's room. I am aghast to be confronted with all the rich persons of the town, when she points to me accusingly, 'This is the only sister against our decision.'

I feel as if in a lions' den. As a means of escape from their roaring, I ask: 'I have a very serious question for you. Every year in the college calendar, a full page is reserved to carry the following statement in block letters: "No Donation or Capitation fee is levied for Admission." As I am in charge of the calendar, can I print this statement this year too?' One of them answers emphatically that we should print the same sentence, saying that we'll be receiving the money soon after the interview by the Principal but just before the admission procedure. I continue performing my duties in silence.

The admissions begin. The highest amount received for a seat is from my cousin who is rich enough to pay more; hence, I don't regret her giving a donation. Soon my batch mate sister's cousin is turned away as they cannot afford to pay the rather big amount of donation that is demanded from them. The sister comes crying to the Principal but to no avail.

The second incident occurs when a former teacher's niece comes for interview. Her family, too, are reluctant to pay the donation, and are treated very harshly by the PTA. The retired teacher slams the present teachers who dash off to the Principal's room. Meeting me on the way, they loudly ask: 'Who gave the PTA the right to scold us? Why do we collect donations for seats? The college is losing its grand reputation by these unfair dealings.' Coolly, I respond: 'None of you have the right to shout now. If ever anyone can speak against this sort of money making, it is me. Weren't you there when this matter was discussed? Why didn't you object to it then? Now I don't think you have the right.'

The matter of donations is all over the media. A TV report says: 'A famous women's college in town is said to be accepting capitation fee for admission. If proved to be true, proper action will be taken to rectify this.' When the time for the degree admissions arrives, the Principal tells us that no donations will be demanded for the seats. It is because an order prohibiting this has been decreed from the Generalate. One morning, two staff members from the deputy director's office in Thrissur come to the college for checking whether money has been received by us for admission. Complaints against the college have reached the director of Collegiate Education, Trivandrum. When students at random are asked whether they have given capitation fee to the college for admission, all reply in the negative as none of them know the meaning of the term 'capitation'. Thus, we all escape from that puddle.

A Retreat team, after praying over the college, concludes that a curse has fallen on it, as the divine message suggests that we are culprits of bribery and gluttony. When I am angrily informed about this, as I am in charge of the Retreat, I tell them: 'You tell this not to me but to your dear sisters who are the authorities here. They are responsible for these happenings.'

How far some sisters can go to satiate their greed is seen at a fund-raiser held in the college. That year, an orchestra team led by the playback singer, Sri K.G. Sreekumar is invited by the college for a performance, to collect funds. One of the benefactors offers a two-wheeler, 'Sunny', to the winner of the lucky draw out of the tickets sold. Buyers are especially reminded not to lose the counterfoils. A circular is issued by the Provincialate prohibiting sisters from selling the tickets. Despite this, the Principal compels us to sell as many tickets as possible. Even though I dislike going around tapping money from people, I too am forced to obey. But Jesus saves me from the unpleasant task. The first day I go out to sell, my foot is badly cut by a broken bottle piece on the road. I am taken to hospital; many stitches are needed and the doctor tells me to rest the foot until they are removed.

Nonetheless, though I am limping about, I get roped into reciting the prayer before the function. There is a bomb threat, and the other sisters suggest that if I recite a prayer in the auditorium before the function starts, everything will be okay! Limping, I climb the stage and recite the prayer. If all have placed trust in my prayer, I am all the more happy.

A very influential and business-minded sister among us succeeds in shifting the norms for getting the two-wheeler, by persuading the Principal. Now the two-wheeler will not go to the 'lucky' one, but to the one who has sold the most number of tickets. Those who have kept the counterfoils of their tickets are fooled by this twist. One of the students in the college had struggled hard and collected a huge amount. All predicted that she would be the winner. But at the last moment, this sister gathers money from many of the sisters, including me, and wins the Sunny. How ironical that though it is laid down that sisters are not to sell the tickets, it is one of them, who as the best seller, gets the key of the vehicle in front of the public and everyone in the Province!

Now I am to have another strange experience at the hands of the authorities. It is time for my promotion and I am called upon to urgently attend a refresher course at Dharwar University in Karnataka which offers a course in English. From our directory, I get the address of a convent nearby and write to them, asking for accommodation for three weeks. I plan to get to Dharwar from Bangalore by Rani Chennamma Express train. My idea is to spend the day when I reach Bangalore in the ladies' waiting room at the railway station and to resume my journey in the evening. But the sisters in the convent suggest I go to one Father's place to rest. I am given the address of a priest who is well known and noted for his celibacy and holiness. I get a prompt reply from Father to my letter of request, assuring me of a 'royal welcome'. The day of departure nears; an uneasiness is rising within me. As usual, I tell Jesus: 'If you don't want me to go for the course, please give me a sign.' The sign comes in the form of a viral fever. I am bedridden, shivering with fever, and suffering from intense body pain and lack of appetite. All my appointments are cancelled. To travel the next day by train to Dharwar seems unthinkable. I wish to tell the Principal to cancel the ticket. But she comes to the sick room instead and first chides me about wasting college money, then impresses how important the promotion is and insists that I go. That is final. The Superior looks at me sympathetically. I can't expect concern like Amma's from anyone here. So somehow, despite the fever, I pull myself together to go, but the question lingers within, 'Why did Jesus tell me not to go?' I get the answer only later.

Reaching Bangalore station early in the morning, I get off the train and see the priest impatiently waiting for me. He is very excited and hugs me, quite unusual for him, given his reticent nature. As promised, 'royally' I am taken to his residence. After breakfast, despite my reluctance, he takes me to Lalbagh. He has a hidden agenda in taking me there, I soon realize. Pointing to each couple beneath the trees, he holds forth on the need for physical love. Then he tells me about cases of priests and Bishops who have illicit relationships with women. There is one Bishop who sleeps with a woman, has a child from her and makes arrangements for its maintenance. I feel terribly awkward at the priest's strange behaviour and manner of talking. Later, I am taken to his room for coffee prepared by him. While I am having the coffee sitting on the cot, the only place in the room to sit, he comes and embraces me hard, almost suffocating me. When I struggle to escape from his clutches, he squeezes my breasts and asks me to show them to him. Refusing him angrily, I get up to leave but he forces me to sit down, asking, 'Have you seen a "man"?' Stunned, I shake my head to say 'no'. In no time, he undresses himself. Now I am curious enough to watch! I have read in novels about this but have never seen one with my own eyes. The moment I see it, I remember Sylvia Plath's novel, *The Bell Jar*, where she describes it as 'the head of a tortoise'. After a while, he shows me a milky liquid oozing from there and lectures me on the 'thousands of lives' it has. Although I resist undressing myself, after repeated persuasion, I oblige, and show him 'a female' on the condition that it will be for the twinkle of an eye. After getting dressed, I am taken to the railway station for the onward journey. Later, I regret the event because I never wanted this to happen. In our convent life, we least expect molestation of this type. Are we not safe even within the Four Walls of Seclusion?

When I get back to the convent, with great hesitation, I tell my closest friend, Sr Maria, what has happened to me. She is rudely shaken, as she knows the priest well. We can't understand how he has changed like this once he moved from Kerala to Bangalore. I feel it is perhaps the metropolitan city culture which is responsible. Sister and I are to give the Holy Communion in the chapel that day, but I am now feeling so unholy that I can't bring myself to go. Sister persuades me to somehow go ahead, and later to seek advice on how to make amends. Meanwhile, that priest tries to pursue me and wants to carry on with me over the telephone, at which point I am forced to slam down the receiver, if he is on the line! He asks me not to confess about what transpired between us to any priest (unless it is him!), or better still, to confess everything directly to God! I carry this burden of guilt within me until a new priest from elsewhere comes to the convent, and I am able to confess everything. Performing penance and some prayers that he suggests, I feel pure again.

The marginalized and the underprivileged need our urgent attention and care. Those students who come without food from home are taken to the hostel mess during the recess. Earlier, there had been a provision of free food for poor students. Gradually, all such charitable deeds came to a standstill, but nevertheless I take them to the mess and ask the sister to give food. Now a new sister, a very stingy one, is in charge of the kitchen. She shouts at me when the poor students are brought. This matter is discussed with the Assistant Warden, Sr Maria, who is very friendly with me. She advises me to get some money from the rich students in my class, buy canteen coupons and send the poor students to the canteen with them.

On one occasion, the chechie of our Sr Ellen needs money for her daughter's marriage. Sr Ellen, who is one of our non-teaching staff, takes her chechie to the Superior. But the Superior refuses to grant the loan of 10,000 rupees. Terribly upset, the sister shares the incident with me. I go to the Superior and get permission to beg for the money among my favourites. In spite of several letters and phone calls, I can raise only very little money for the cause. Only then do I turn to

Jesus: 'Lord, you have plenty of money to spare. They are in need of at least 10,000 rupees. Can't you arrange for it?' A few days later, when I am busy helping the office people, a teacher calls me urgently to the veranda. I get a little irritated as she is persistent, but reluctantly I go. 'Sister Jesme, do you know anyone facing financial problems for performing a marriage?' I am shocked. 'Why do you ask so, Miss?'

'My husband works in collaboration with a German company which offers 10,000 rupees annually for a poor couple's marriage. Last year, we lost the chance as we couldn't find a deserving pair. This year's is about to lapse.'

'Miss, Jesus brought you to me.' I point out the couple, get the money myself, with the permission of the Principal, and give it to them through the sister.

On another occasion, a poor student of mine needs 500 rupees to remit fees for an exam. To go to the exam centre, she needs another hundred rupees, a total of 600 altogether. I turn to Jesus and wait for the miracle. My spiritual son had been giving 200 rupees every month for a poor student's study but stopped after one year. But one evening, he comes after 6 p.m. to the convent to meet me. I am cross as meeting visitors after 6 p.m. is against the convent rules. He insists that if he does not meet me that very day, he may use the money he has brought with him and wants to hand over to me. It is exactly 600 rupees! 'Mon, why do you give me money now? Your term is over.' He replies, 'Sister, I saw a piece about you in the papers by one of your students. Then I remembered that I have stopped helping the poor through you. This money you can spend for someone in need.'

'Mon, Jesus has sent you to me. I had asked Him for exactly six hundred rupees.'

How poor students get pushed around, even in convents, is driven home to me. One year, for the pre-degree economics exam, the questions are all out of syllabus. The students can't answer any of the questions. When the staff members assemble for the centralized valuation camp, they object to evaluating the papers. Hence, the university is forced to conduct another exam. As wide publicity is not given to the re-exam, many of the students can't write it. This includes daughters of some noted people. So the university has to conduct the exam for a third time. This is given wide publicity through all types of media, including the radio. Before the result of this exam is published, the university declares the last date of admissions for BA. At this point, a poor girl named Rosy goes to the admission office and asks: 'Chechie, I haven't yet got my marks for economics. Then how shall I submit my application form before the last date?' The chechie is sarcastic: 'You bring the application form only when you get all the marks.' She hasn't heard about the three exams conducted by the university. The girl, naturally, goes home, waits for the marks to be published, and brings the completed form. Now the admission's office refuses to accept the form as it is late. She comes to me, as her tutor, and shows me the mark-list. A very quiet girl she is, who rarely speaks to the teachers, including me. I am overjoyed to see her marks in economics. Girls getting lesser marks than her have already been admitted to the course. Hence, I tell her to submit her form to the admission office. But they refuse to accept.

Reaching the admission office, I tell the sisters: 'Why don't you accept it? She has got good marks. Anyway, our seats are not filled. Can't you keep the form by marking "late" on it? I have seen you doing so before.' Realizing the logic of the argument, they accept the form. After two days, a student is sent to Rosy's house asking her to join the next day, and pay the fees. Her family does not have enough money, so they borrow a gold ring from the neighbour and pawn it for fees and the travel expenses. The day she is asked to join, I have urgent business elsewhere and am on leave. When I get back, I hear that Rosy and her father were sent away by the Principal without allowing her to join. I cannot control my anger—she dares to play only with poor people like Rosy. I meet the Principal and ask for the reason for not admitting her. She asserts her authority and is adamant, even as I try my level best to explain the plight of Rosy and her family.

Meeting the Mother Provincial, I explain the present predicament. Rosy lives in a hilly forest area with her parents. Her father is a goatherd and earns a living from goat's milk and meat. It is a wasteland—no edible fruits or crops grow there. No electricity is supplied there. No postman will climb to the heights of her house; he leaves the letters in the shop below. Only when someone climbs down in the mornings, do they get letters. No newspaper boy would risk coming up daily. Then how do they keep in touch with the world outside? There lies the beauty of the family's success in overcoming their harsh circumstances. The father listens daily to the news broadcast on the battery-operated transistor. That the university exam will be conducted for the third time was announced over the radio. That's how he came to know about it. The second daughter lost her chance of admission to a job-oriented course as they did not get the interview card on time. Now the eldest may also lose her chance to study. How will they retrieve the pawned gold ring and return it to the neighbour? A heart of stone would have melted, but not that of my authorities'. The Mother Provincial replies, 'I agree with what you say. But I can't tell the Principal to admit her. As she is a coward, she may not be daring enough to admit the girl.' I don't understand this logic. I respond, 'If you can't solve this problem and rescue a poor girl, let me adopt my methods.' Anyway, I ask her for her blessings.

I leave the Provincialate determined to do something to save the future of this poor, deserving girl. I am lucky to meet a priest-advocate in connection with an NSS residential camp. He understands the gravity of the situation and offers help. He makes an appointment with the Principal. He is convinced that if we go to court, definitely the girl will get admission. The court will always be in favour of an individual rather than an institution. Next day, the advocate meets the Principal but again she argues and tries to find some loophole. Only after his warning, does she agree to admit her on the last day of admissions. To make sure she actually gets admission—and since in all this she has missed a month's classes—I ask the teachers if they have any objection to her listening to their lectures from the veranda outside. They are only too happy to teach someone like her. Knowing that all are behind Rosy, the Principal sends her a message through an attender that she can join the following day. Rosy becomes a degree holder after three years. Then she dedicates one year to service in the SOS Village for the orphans there.

Usually the senior-most sisters are made warden; when Sr Lithia and I are eligible, Sr Jimsa, who is close to the Principal and much junior to us, is surreptitiously taken to the hostel at night when we are away and is declared warden the next morning. Naturally, Sr Jimsa is haughty with us. She insists upon bringing in a rule that without a local guardian, no student can stay in the hostel. Once the parents of a girl named Alice approach me, saying that their daughter has got admission, but cannot gain entry into the hostel because of this rule. Discussing the situation, Alice's father enquires about my family members and gets to know my sister's name. I joke about this with the Principal and warden. The next thing I know in the evening is that my sister has been appointed as the local guardian of Alice, without asking me. The girl is harassed by the warden as she has some connection with me. For an event, my family decides to take Alice home. Getting permission from the warden, Amma comes to the hostel but Alice has already gone out to the tuition centre, so she picks her up from there.

One morning, the Mother Provincial comes to the convent along with Sr Jimsa who had spent the previous night in the Provincialate. The Provincial 'cross-questions' me on the complaints she has received from Sr Jimsa. One accusation is that I dine in the kitchen with the kitchen maids, though we are not supposed to mingle with them so as to keep up our 'dignity' as sisters. Another complaint is that Alice was taken away from the tuition centre without permission. I have a tough time defending myself. Later, the Provincial comes to realize the exact situation and all the incidents against me are found to be concocted.

An unfortunate incident takes place in the hostel. A girl comes for counselling, to save her friend from a snare. On asking, I come to know that her friend, a brilliant girl, has lost her mother and has started regarding a senior girl as her mother figure. The friend is now lagging in her studies because in all her free time she is with the senior girl. The senior actually plays the role of the mother; she even 'breastfeeds' the 'daughter' for hours. Desperately, I realize that this is occurring in my niece's room, as the girl is her room-mate. My niece is terribly upset. As the academic year is ending, I dare not enter into the 'mother-daughter' relationship. Besides, how can I inform the warden about it? Also, since only a few more days are left for them to leave the hostel for Revision holidays, I ask my niece to adjust. Meanwhile, I inform the girl's father about the situation and ask him to keep an eye on his daughter. At least he should know what has happened here and the shock she has experienced. Later, I hear she had trouble in her marital life, and her father wisely provided her with psychiatric treatment. The psychiatrist told the girl's father that the hostel incident had affected her intensely.

Certain convictions regarding 'suffering' guide my life. I have decided never to say 'no' to Jesus. Whatever He gives as suffering, I am willing to endure. If I reach a point where I cannot bear it any longer, I tell Him that I can endure no more and He should stop. Very rarely do I need to ask this of Him. The sufferings are invariably followed by a stream of His grace. When a channel is dug in an arid land, the earth suffers great pain; but eventually, it is only through this channel that life-giving water reaches the land. We need to gather sufferings as precious jewels. And if I have gained some depth in my life, it is because of the ordeals I have gone through; intense suffering really makes one a 'doctorate' in that field! Such a person can guide those enduring similar sufferings. The Epistle exhorts: 'God comforts us to make us comforters.' I can console those who have undergone the ordeal of the Land Injunction, for we have gone through it ourselves; the families who suffer loss of their beloved ones either by way of murder or suicide can be provided solace as we have ourselves experienced such sorrows. The joys and sorrows of the rich, the poor, the lower middle class, and the upper middle class are well known to us as we have passed through all this ourselves.

When one day a girl comes dashing into my room and breaks down because her father called her a prostitute, I am reminded of my own Appan. There was a time when he hated me because I was defending Amma. He came drunk one night, and seeing me asleep, called me a harlot. I heard his words in a sleepy haze and they remained with me. Perhaps to give solace to this girl who wants to become a nun!

My freedom with Jesus is limitless. I share everything with Him, even my innermost secrets, my weaknesses, failures, and the wrong deeds in mind and action. I dare to be angry with Him, even obstinate at times; and once I even decided to have a tiff with Him. But the next moment, when a phone call comes, automatically I turn to Him and say, let this one not bring any problems. This is repeated a few times and finally I tell Him: 'O! Jesus, let us compromise. I can't live without talking to you.' This makes me say to all that what Emerson said is true. If I have the 'divine majority' with Jesus on my side, I am not afraid of the thousands against me.

4

BRAVING THE CRAZY WAVES

I am now transferred to Amala College. My stint there is hectic and will bring me great joy but also deep anguish and despair, which will almost break me. But to begin with, barely have I joined when I am given the charge of the Jesus Youth Convention to be held in the college after a few months. The Jesus Youth Movement is the outcome of the Charismatic Renewal in the Church during the twentieth century. And the movement is rather well established in Amala College.

Every weekend, I take the students for the Whole Night Adoration at the Retreat Centre, named Madonna Sehiona. Some of my duties for the convention include collecting money to meet the expenses; conducting core-group and general prayers; preparing decorations for the auditorium; getting the chapel ready for the three days' Adoration; and publicizing the event, to draw in as many participants as possible. Some days before the opening, there is day-night practice of the orchestra in our auditorium. The food for the hundreds attending the convention is prepared by the youths themselves. As they cook through the night, they need water and electricity. The electrician is made to stay over for operating the generator and the motor. But when the power fails, no one is to be seen. I have to run around looking for the electrician. The youth turn to me alone for everything. Even the sisters who are asked by the Principal to assist me get their sleep. But I have to toil hard for what is a thankless task.

I get involved in the events at the college. An exposition of the political and social history of India is planned by the Principal; students from other colleges too will be visiting us for this. We are all looking forward to the event comprising talks by good speakers. The work of decorating the auditorium is allotted to a sister who has been at Amala College for years. I and another teacher are supposed to help her. But when the day of the event approaches, I suddenly find myself dumped with the entire job. I am rushing around until the last moment to arrange everything and am unable to participate in a single talk or function. On all such occasions when I am forsaken by others, they remark that I am talented enough to do things all alone!

There are also other functions where I am in demand. At Dolour's Church, it is decided to convene a meeting for youth, Basilica Youth Movement (BYM). To guide the proceedings, the Vicar and his assistants plan to have a priest and a sister preferred by the youth. Even though I am now in Amala, most of the boys and girls suggest my name. When the Vicar, later the Archbishop, wants me to take charge for the three days of the convention, while staying at St Maria's, I cannot but accept. But naturally, this too creates 'jealousy' as there are numerous convents in the parish and none of the sisters from there are selected.

The status of the younger sisters in the convent becomes apparent in the Provincial Synaxis. This is an official assembly of the elected nuns, which has the authority to change rules, create new ones and to elect the Provincial and the Council. It is held every three years and its members are elected from among the professed sisters. The junior sisters have one representative elected from among themselves. That year, I am selected to be a member among the senior sisters.

During the Synaxis, all the younger sisters remain mum throughout the discussions, so that they will be considered docile and be again elected the next time around. Even though the others warn me, I decide to speak whenever the Holy Spirit inspires. The first day I listen to long-winded speeches, going nowhere—an utter waste of time and energy. The majority of the speeches by the speakers are aimed at garnering votes for themselves or their favourites to get elected to the Provincial Council. There is no genuine desire to seek the Will of God. The Holy Spirit is far away from this arena! One long discussion is about whether or not there is a need for an additional councillor to manage spiritual affairs. A sister asks for explanation, but everyone who gets up to speak goes round and round, never touching upon the question. Towards the end, I raise my hand to speak, but am ignored. The younger sisters are seated behind the senior ones, to indirectly indicate that we belong to the 'second row'. Not being given the mike, I loudly begin to explain that 'In the Bible—"The Acts of the Apostles"—

there is a reference to a similar situation. When the disciples see that they are not able to perform charitable deeds like giving alms, helping widows and so on, due to lack of time, they entrust such tasks to the deacons who are the virtuous men among the followers. They realize they should devote themselves to the most important duty of preaching the Gospel. Here the situation is just the other way around. As the Provincial and the normal councillors are engaged in administrative affairs, they don't get enough time to preach the Gospel and look after the spiritual matters of the sisters. Hence, there arises the need for an additional spiritual councillor.' After this explanation, all are convinced.

Another issue on which I intervene during this assembly is regarding the punishment of a sister, who is the headmistress of a school, for her disobedience. Hours pass in discussion without reaching any conclusion. Can sisters be so cruel, I wonder. Then I get up and speak: 'Can't we think of any method of greater love to win over this sister instead of punishing her? How many times have you all tried to punish me in various ways? That will make things worse. Only by more love, can anyone be subdued. Think of that troublesome sister, who is now one of the best, because of the authorities' concern for her. Can we all take a decision to love this sister more and thus transform her?' The suggestion is accepted also by the Superior of her convent. Strangely, after all this, I am never elected to the Synaxis again. There might be other reasons. But it seems the authorities do not want the younger sisters to come out and speak openly, but to pretend to be meek.

Meanwhile, I have gone to Prof. R.V. for the second time to get registered for the Ph.D programme under him. I am looking forward to doing research again. With his help, a project outline is prepared, submitted, and I get registered as a research candidate. The UGC has proposed a Faculty Improvement Programme for research scholars for the new Plan period. As I have got registered, I am asked to apply. Filling up the form and getting recommendations from my Supervisor, I submit my doctoral proposal on 'The narratological study of the fictional works of Ruskin Bond', for the scrutiny by the committee convened for this purpose by the Principal. After the meeting, I ask Sr Marylit, the one in charge of liaising with the UGC, my rank in the order of selection. She is surprised and tells me that I am selected. The UGC instructs the university to prepare a panel in order of merit. Sr Marylit is entrusted with this task.

But it isn't going to be smooth sailing. There is a row before I can actually join. Due to some carelessness by her in preparing the list of names, no one is recommended for the FIP in the first year. I lose eleven months' leave. When the committee meets a few months later, I am not favoured by the head of the department as I had availed of this scheme for my M. Phil. When the Principal is adamant, I fight back and threaten to file a case, if they do not follow the rules, according to which I should be ranked first. I would never do any such thing, of course. Now I have to settle my leave problem. I have availed of the leave I am eligible for, but the FIP is not in sight. The guest faculty, my ex-student, has already been teaching, so the Principal wants her to continue. The office can find no solution. The Principal throws up her hands, saying it is not for her to decide on the nature of anyone's leave. God intervenes at this point and I am allowed to join the FIP by the Directorate of College Development Council without much delay.

When I next come to the convent, the Principal purposely avoids me. I haven't done anything against her, so I too just ignore her. Unlike earlier, this time I leave without saying goodbye. Then I happen to watch a movie, *Summer in Bethlehem*, with my friend Susmitha. In the movie, the character of Suresh Gopi exhorts that of Manju Warrier not to waste time trying to find out who her parents are. Like her, he is an orphan. There is only one life for them, he says. 'Let us give happiness to others as much as we can.' I am moved by this thought. The next day, I reach the convent but the Principal has gone to the Provincialate. I call and ask her pardon for leaving like that. Happy and at peace now, I return to my research.

There are six of us doctoral scholars in the department—five men and me. We are great friends and a lot of leg-pulling goes on amongst us. Even the professors in the department, and especially my supervisor, are infected by our spiritedness. 'Where is "Panchali"?' he enquires jocularly of the others— whom he calls the 'Panchpandavas'! Many evenings, we go to the beach and spend hours discussing and chatting. Besides, we arrange an excursion trip of the whole department, which is great fun.

I am particularly lucky to have Prof. R.V. as my supervisor again. He is a genius and a source of great intellectual inspiration, a confidante in crucial situations, a comrade in times of fun and enjoyment, and a friend in all times of need. Humble in his brilliance, he keeps away from the power games and petty politics in the department. During the release function for his book, attended by literary celebrities, I am overwhelmed by his gesture of coming down to me in the audience with a copy.

After submitting the thesis within the stipulated time of two years, I come back to rejoin Amala College. Little to nothing has changed—the two warring factions, as old as the college, are still there, and pervade all college activities. The Vice-Principal and the Principal each belongs to a faction. They rarely speak to each other, and like the Opposition party in politics, the Vice-Principal is against all the deeds of the Principal and her group. When the Principal retires and the next one takes office, her group gains power and privilege. Sisters of the other group take a long leave, either for higher studies or for some religious course.

It is the duty of the Vice-Principal to conduct the College Day and the Principal's farewell ceremony. I get pulled in as mediator, given the friction between the two parties. The Vice-Principal, Sr Deena, gets the assistance of an artist to put up a performance for Rs 25,000, a huge amount those days. I am not for it because of the money involved. Without being aware of this, the Principal goes ahead on her own to make arrangements—unmindful of the fact that she cannot be conducting her own farewell! Terribly upset and angry, the Vice-Principal complains to me, as I am the next in seniority. I suggest an easy way out. The students are good dancers, and the stage is also suitable for dance items. 'Why not have choreographic presentations of a few songs on Mother Mary, Sister?' There is a cassette by a priest known to me, comprising sweet songs on Mother Mary and I can get his permission to use them. My Vice-Principal is relieved but as the suggestion has come from me, I end up with the duty of preparing the item.

At the time of handover, there is another crisis. The Principal wants to meet the Vice-Principal, Sr Deena, in person, and waits in office for her the whole morning. I happen to pass by. The Principal is terribly upset and wants to tear up the handover note. When I rush to the convent to persuade Sr Deena, she breaks down and tells me, 'Jesme, you don't know how she treated me all these years. I cannot forgive or forget. How can I meet her now?' The Superior's attempt to advise her fails and only upsets her more. 'Don't compel me in this matter. I won't go to her.' And we know that it is final. After a certain time, the Principal rips the note apart and comes to the convent, but out of good nature, comes to talk to Sr Deena: 'Sr Deena, tomorrow I am leaving. May God help you to discharge your duties well!' I smile at the Principal with admiration. At least she has shown that much graciousness.

As Sr Deena becomes the Principal, I am to assist her as the Vice-Principal. Soon I am asked: 'Memy, to which party do you belong?' They mean the two warring groups in the convent as well as in the college. The teachers call me 'Memy' as I was their student. Innocently, I reply pointing above: 'To neither of the parties; but to the "Party Above".'

'Then, Memy, be prepared to suffer. No party will save you from trouble.' I assure them that I believe I have 'the Divine Majority'.

Sr Deena in her first address to the college tells that she will follow the footsteps of the former Principal and all her policies will be continued. But when the former Principal comes to the college in order to sign some documents, Sr Deena avoids her, not caring to either talk to her or invite her to the Principal's room. This happens once again when she is invited by the college to inaugurate its Union. I am the last person to know about it and try to suggest other speakers. The next day, the former Principal calls me to complain about suggesting her name to the students for the inauguration. The Provincial Councillor has scolded her for going to the college, saying that it is a plot hatched by me, in order to belittle the present Principal. The Union members want to justify my position, but I dissuade them for the sake of maintaining peace in the campus.

The Vice-Principal is the treasurer of the PTA in the college. Hence, I have to maintain the record of the accounts. I find that I am expected to make false entries. During meetings, the Principal often stamps on my foot, to tell me to be silent. I am always in tears because of the accounts being topsy-turvy. She wants to tackle any resulting problems by devious methods— hiding the actual amount from the parents and teachers.

Much secrecy is maintained regarding official matters. Any project offered by the UGC or circulars from the government, are kept highly confidential. By constant postponing, the Principal tries to evade many of the issues she faces. Escapism is the secret of her mental peace. But there are also potential seeds of revenge dormant in her. To wreak vengeance on Sr Claudia and her followers in the English department, she humiliates the present staff. Being Vice-Principal and belonging to the English department, the staff members come to me with their grievances, but my attempts to solve the problems are exercises in futility.

A proposal for a grant amounting to Rs 200,000 is to be submitted to the University during every Plan period. Our department has been receiving the grant in previous years. The condition for renewal is that the department should have six valid publications within the last five years. With more than thirty of my publications and those of the others, we have around forty in all. But the circular is not shown to the staff as yet. Even though I am the Vice-Principal, a matter regarding my department is not conveyed to me. Hurriedly, some teacher is asked to jot down the year's publications, and the proposal is sent with a list of six of them instead of forty. One article is found to be substandard by the UGC and the department loses the grant. The Principal and Sr Marylit are pleased at this rejection, not thinking for a moment about the overall loss to the college.

When I ask the Principal whether there is another chance, she says, 'The file is already closed.' When I meet the director in Bangalore, to follow up, I learn that he expected the staff to discuss such proposals for over a month and he had no idea that we came to know about them only the previous day. He says, 'I wonder at your Principal; not a word did she utter. But Sr Marylit is smart. Why did she do this? I had told them to come in the days that followed, if anything had to be rectified. Why didn't they tell you that? Now the committee has dispersed. Alone I can do nothing.' When we plead with him, all he can say is, 'Submit the proposal again when the provision for minor grants comes. Then let me consider the matter.' Meanwhile, he wants me to convey to Sr Marylit that he is angry with her.

When the Principal attends the 'Forty Days' Prayer', once optional, but now compulsory for all the CMC sisters, I have to take charge as Principal. This prayer is inspired by Moses, who spent forty days on Mount Sinai before God bestowed him with the tablets of the Ten Commandments. Jesus, before he entered the public ministry, too, spent forty days in prayer. I have to perform multiple duties: as chief examiner; as assistant in the International Film Festival organized by Gargi (a Women Media Collective) in collaboration with Chetana Media Institute; as chief coordinator of the first campus film of Amala College called *Jaalakangal*, of eight minutes duration; besides as Principal-in-charge.

The experience of the campus film coordination is exciting— but also frustrating. *Jaalakangal* is a tender story about an affluent lady who remains confined to a luxurious room. She is cut off from nature, either out of her own volition or due to the restriction her class position places on her. It is raining and she wishes to step outside, but can't. She looks out of the window and sees a small girl playing in the rain, dancing, making paper boats and watching them gliding in the stream of water. As there is only music in the background, the girl symbolizes either the lady's nostalgic memories of her childhood, or her dream to be a child once again. At another level, it would suggest that a poor girl can be free in nature, whereas there are taboos for a woman of 'fashionable affectations'.

Within a week, the script is discussed and drafted, and the heroine and other actors are chosen; we have reserved the 'student-package' for the Camera–Editing–Dubbing (Production) Unit from the Film Chetana Media Institute, and the locations and sets have been prepared. Now the rehearsals are in progress. But a serious problem arises when the eight-year-old child actor refuses to remove her petticoat for shooting. She is to appear in panties. When I share the problem with a staff member, a friend, she asks: 'Memy, why stick to "set-frames"? Why can't you incorporate such "out-of-the-frame" shots into the film?' Her suggestion triggers my imagination and changes my approach to the problem. Shots—out of frame—of the film's director, the child's own mother and the heroine trying to persuade the child to remove the petticoat and appear in panties are now included as part of the film. The heroine comes up with an interesting line of persuasion: 'Haven't you seen grown-up chechies wearing short dresses in the movies?' At the age of eight, a girl is reluctant to remove her petticoat. But as she grows up, she is eager to cast off even the clothes necessary to preserve her modesty. What is society doing to our girls, I wonder. How do they get transformed like this?

Then there are other problems from within while making the film. None of the sisters cooperate, despite my being the Principal-in-charge. Even though the film is released by the Mayor, the sisters are reluctant to attend. At least to recite a prayer, I invite a sister. I tell her, 'Even though you are against films, you are not against reciting a prayer, I suppose.' She leaves the place soon after the prayer. Despite all these difficulties,

I am elated because of the presence of sincere and hardworking attenders and workers who assist me in the venture. Moreover, I am satisfied at the audience comprising hostellers, parents, teachers and a few day scholars, who all actively participate in the heated discussion following the screenings. A PTA member, who is a businessman, does not like the film. 'Why not make more direct films like *Chemmeen*,' he asks. Someone else does not want women to be always represented as weeping. But the film receives recognition at the Gargi festival, gets a consolation prize from the film critics, and an award of Rs 1,000 in a competition held at the engineering college, Thrissur.

Films remain for me an important activity and a medium of communicating His message even when I later become the Principal of another college. If we are to look beyond the letters of the laws laid down for our Congregation, and for the Church in general, we need such new mediums.

During this time, I get news of my supervisor's incurable illness. On a Saturday, I take leave and spend two days assisting his family in the hospital. On Sunday, he leaves this world and I sit beside his lifeless body along with his wife, son and daughter-in-law. I am immensely grateful to my Lord for allowing me to render this last service to him, as a token of my love and respect.

Let me now dwell on our Vow of Obedience. Nowadays, sisters are trained to preach at Retreats, and conduct spiritual courses which until lately were the exclusive domain of the priests. Of course, the sisters selected for this purpose are only the 'goody-goody' or 'holy' ones. A sister comes to our convent to speak on the fervour and spirituality of the Blessed Chavara, our Founder. 'Dear sisters! Ponder upon the obedience of our Founder! He demands unconditional obedience from the sisters of his Congregation, CMC. When our sisters in the past were asked to plant a stem upside down, they obeyed and by the miracle of God, it sprouted because of their blind obedience.' This is an oft-quoted example, and our spontaneous response to this is that 'the stem might be that of tapioca' which sprouts on both sides! Listening to this cliché, I intervene: 'Sister, in this ultra-modern age, why do you still lecture on "blind obedience"? Think of the junior sisters who listen to your age-old notions. Recently, we were asked to develop "responsible obedience", discarding "blind obedience". But how can you still emphasize on the past explanations?' 'Responsible obedience' involves understanding the pulse from the context and then asking the sisters to obey. Sister affirms, 'Jesme, I have to repeat what I said. This is what our Founder has said, even though years back. How can I teach something different from what he had preached and written?' I find this logic unacceptable and pose a counter-question. 'Sister, I'm reminded of our Apostle, St Paul, who has said women must not speak in public. How dare we, sisters, even preach in public or in front of groups! Oughtn't we to do exactly as he has said, because he is the Apostle?' She sits down dumbfounded and embarrassed.

Christ's Way, later called Christianity, is Eastern in its origin; Jesus gave women due status in His lifetime. On many occasions, He uplifted women in the most commendable way. His first missionary was the Woman of Samaria at the well, who is said to have had relationships with more than five men. His constant followers in the Way of the Cross and at the foot of the Cross were women. It was to Mary Magdalene that the Lord first appeared after He had risen from the dead. But as Christianity travelled to what we now call the 'Western' world, the West's ideas, customs and perspectives coloured the religion. Especially St Paul's, who never married, and spoke against the prominence of women in the Church:

> I desire that . . . women should adorn themselves modestly and sensibly in seemly apparel, not with braided hair or gold or pearls or costly attire . . . Let a woman learn in silence with all submissiveness. I permit no woman to teach or to have authority over men; she is to keep silent. For Adam was formed first, then Eve; and Adam was not deceived, but the woman was deceived and became a transgressor. Yet woman will be saved through bearing children, if she continues in faith and love and holiness, with modesty. [1Timothy 2: 8-15.]

I admit that St Paul is the most spiritual of Apostles but his anti-woman attitude is lamentable. This tradition of belittling woman has continued in the Church till date. Attempts to redeem her status happen in writing but very rarely in convictions or deeds. Lay people ask, why do the priests have more freedom than the sisters? My only answer is that there still exists discrimination against women in the local Church. The priests travel and go for movies in lay dress, officiate or attend weddings, and even consume liquor. Their financial status is quite sound. But nuns cannot dream of all these things. Priesthood is believed to be based on the teachings of Jesus and those of the Church. The ceremony of anointing a priest is one of the sacraments of the Church, whereas the ceremony of the women taking vows and entering the convent is not accepted as a sacrament. We are not permitted to officiate at the Holy Mass or hear Confession. The 'office' (Prayer for the Dead) recited by the priests was allowed to be used by us till recently; but now, a different prayer is laid down for recitation for lay people and the sisters.

While confessing, a priest asks me: 'When you go for movies either with the students or with your colleagues, do you wear the sister's gown?'

'Yes, Father.'

'Sister, is it written in your Constitution that you shouldn't go for movies?'

'No, Father.'

'Is it written in the Constitution of the CMI Fathers that they shouldn't take liquor?'

'I don't know, Father.'

'Yes, it is written so. If they violate it, they should confess. But you needn't, when you see movies.'

People wonder at a sister in the habit and a priest in the lay man's dress participating in programmes and discussions on films. But spirituality has nothing to do with the type of dress one wears. Nowhere is it laid down that sisters should not go for movies, and should only be dressed in the habit. In 1999, during a refresher course in Hyderabad, I went with my fellow students to see *Kuch Kuch Hota Hai*. One of my course mates, a Malayali at that, was terribly upset at my joining them, since I was wearing the habit. For him, my being interested in the film somehow meant disrespect to the habit. Daring to attend such events in my nun's dress might have speeded up my fall from the good books of the religious authorities. But my cause has been the freedom that the women and the nuns should have, along with the men and the priests; I also want to prove that films are not detrimental to spirituality, instead they deepen it. (Films like *Vadakramam*, which I will talk about later.) This belief is carried over and finds expression at St Maria's College where I go next.

The Principal of St Maria's College is about to retire. One of the councillors sounds me out on whether I have any objection to becoming the Principal of a small college. I protest. 'Sister, what do you mean by "small"? She [the college] is the Mother of Amala College and later of many more colleges; the eldest daughter is given in marriage by forsaking all the valuables of the Mother, comprising money, land, books, furniture, and above all, good teachers. Even though richer, the eldest daughter still remains a daughter.' I am soon transferred to St Maria's.

The first thing I do on entering the Principal's office is to place a picture of Jesus before me, on the wall facing me—I call it my 'tabernacle'—and another one just behind me, in the line of vision of my visitors. At all times, I can share with Him my joy, grief, frustration, anger, and what not! He gives me courage in times of troubles and consoles me often. All my queries are directed towards Him and immediately He responds.

The sisters at St Maria's are waiting to see what vengeance I will wreak on Sr Jimsa, now that I am in power. For the past two years, she hasn't been treated well by the previous Principal. I want to take a 'noble revenge' by giving her more love and power. In the sisters' gathering on the very first day, I declare, 'I need two Vice-Principals here for the smooth running of the college. So I need Sr Jimsa as my Vice-Principal, besides Sr Meslin.' The sisters are thunderstruck. They expected just the opposite to happen. I explain, 'If I do the same as what she has done to me, then what is the difference between us?' The decision turns out to be wise. Sr Meslin is one of those who is unable to take even the smallest decision either in an emergency or in normal times; Sr Jimsa is the big pessimist whereas Sr Meslin is the other extreme. I can take a decision, a realistic one, somewhere in between.

In my inaugural talk, I explain to the students: 'I would like to give you as much freedom as you want, provided you are also that responsible. "Freedom with Responsibility"—that is my policy. I am going to open wide the portals of this college. Men and women may interact in the auditorium and the campus. You live in a society comprising both. Learn from now on how to treat the opposite sex. A lack of responsibility will lead to this freedom being curtailed. That is, please don't misuse the freedom given to you.'

The majority of the sisters do not appreciate my stand. Many are non-teaching sisters, and even those who are not are as conservative as the rest and are suspicious of any democracy for the students, but they do not openly oppose me because I am the Principal now. The sister-teachers are also resentful because any change will mean more work for them.

A 'sharing box' is kept in the campus for the students to freely drop their suggestions, without giving names. Every week, I respond to them either in the General Assembly or through the student representatives and Union members. Reading the comments and criticisms, I come to appreciate the students' sense of humour, frankness and prudence. Genuine requests are met promptly. Once I learn through these slips that because of the rainy season, the verandas are slippery and some students have hurt themselves. The slip says, 'If you want to meet your students, come to the hospital—we go there for our fractures and sprains.' Coir carpets are immediately bought and spread in the verandas.

It is a bad time for the college as the visiting NAAC team gives it only a low grade. NAAC (National Assessment and Accreditation Council) is a UGC body for rating colleges, universities and professional institutions. The non-existent clubs, the sloth and the lethargy of the faculty and staff, the lack of incentive for creativity, and so on, have led to the college being down-graded in the two years of the previous administration— or rather non-administration. I don't see the zeal one expects in a college worthy of a visit by a NAAC team. Not a single UGC project has the college applied for so far. A big department, running a postgraduate course, doesn't have a single Ph.D or researcher among its staff members. I have to endeavour to raise the standards to that of a notable college. The problem is an outcome of the management never wanting this college to do better than Amala College, whose retired principals are on our board.

In the first few months of my becoming Principal, I have to deal with administrative irregularities. There is a gherao by the outgoing students of the Computer Science department. Their demand is for the returning of the full amount of their caution deposit. It's a genuine demand as the transfer certificate has already been issued to the students, which suggests that nothing more is due to the college. On enquiry, I learn that without the students' consent, as per the order of the previous Principal, a good amount of the deposit has been deducted before being returned. When a staff member and the parents of a student approach me with this problem, I plead with the former Principal to permit me to return the amounts. She agrees to increase the amount to be returned, but the students and parents will settle for nothing less than the total amount. The matter reaches the university and I am questioned. I repeatedly request the Manager to permit me to return the full amount. The Provincial councillor argues that it is the right of the management to take the money and that I am not to interfere in such matters. Ultimately, on the deputy director's intervention, the councillor relents and allows me to return the full amount to the students. I am stumped when later I learn from the deputy director that the management was blaming me, as the Principal, for the problem. He cautions me that even if I am slapped with a case, I should not expect the Manager to come to my rescue. All I can say to that is, 'I have no other way but to obey.'

In another instance, I come to know that an additional amount of Rs 32,000 is being exacted from each candidate occupying the 'management seat'. Twelve seats in microbiology and biotechnology have been filled this way. The amount is smaller than in other colleges, but I am absolutely against this policy. At Amala College when an additional fee is fixed for non-traditional courses—i.e., courses run without financial commitment to the government—many sisters suggested getting donation for the management seats. (There are traditional, non-traditional and self-financing courses at the university.) As Vice-Principal at Amala, I strongly argued against it: 'If a single rupee is levied for such seats, it is capitation fee.' My conscience taunts me now at the thought of demanding an extra amount. I discuss the matter with the Vice-Principal and the senior sisters. They argue that the Manager insisted upon charging this amount and they just obeyed. I share my dilemma with a priest, in confidence, when he suggests making a separate account and receipt for them under the head, 'Merit cum Means Fund'; at least the amounts will be accounted for and can be distributed among intelligent but poorer students. I am proud of Amala College. But later I learn, that during the time of another Principal after me, huge amounts of money were exacted from parents for admissions. I can only despair.

I have been an advocate of women's equality and freedom, something which has always upset the convent authorities. One day, I get a call from I. Gopinathan (Gopi), a social worker, inviting me to release the book, *Oru Laingika Thozhilaliyude Aatmakadha* (The Autobiography of a Sex Worker), which tells the story of Smt. Nalini Jameela. After arguing for a while, as he asks me to take it as a 'challenge', I agree. Some months earlier, I had shared the stage with her at the Sahitya Akademi and the Gargi (Women Media Collective) officials. When I share my fear with Deedi Damodaran, a film script writer and a social worker who works with women, about how the sisters will react to my decision, she asks me if I will quit the stage where Sri Kunjalikuty presides. His name is connected with the ice-cream parlour sex scandal involving a girl, Regina. This exhortation gives me strength to face any objection from the sisters. When Fr Benny hears about the release of the book, he cautions me: 'Are you aware of what you are doing, Jesme? Or has anyone tricked you into it?'

'Consciously, I have accepted the invitation, Father.'

'Have you got enough points to speak about?' concerned, he presses. I reassure Father again that every day Jesus has been instructing me and giving me courage.

I know a Jesus who has been with tax collectors and harlots. I know Him as one who says, 'I came not to call the righteous, but sinners.'[Mark 2:17b] I know a Saviour who has gone after the Lost Sheep leaving the other ninety-nine in the desert. [Matthew 18:12.] I know the Risen Lord who first appeared to Mary Magdalene, asking: 'Woman, why are you weeping?'[John 20:15] I know a Guru who has taught us to hate sin but love sinners. I may not imbibe the spirit of Nalini, as I have my own convictions, but I love her as a woman who has undergone suffering. This occasion is seen by me as one to preach the all-embracing Love of Jesus, His mercy, His forgiveness and understanding. If I can be proud of a Jesus who challenged hard-hearted men about to stone to death a woman caught at adultery, saying, 'Let him who is without sin among you be the first to throw a stone at her.' [John 8:7] I am fit enough to release Nalini's book. As a teacher of literature, I teach Bernard Shaw's *Mrs. Warren's Profession* without shame. A literary work is a contribution to society and is to be honoured. Besides, as I notice that Gopi co-authors the book, I would like to ask, who wants a woman to remain a sex worker? Is it the need of a male chauvinistic section of the society?

The evening before the function, the news of my releasing the book becomes public through a TV channel. The Mother Provincial is furious: 'Who are you to gift this book to the public? What do you mean by this? Have you fallen into a trap?' I firmly tell her, 'No, Mother. I have accepted the offer with full awareness. I consider this to be the apt occasion to speak about the mercy and love of Jesus.' She is aghast and emphatically affirms, 'The Provincial Council decides that you should not go.' The Vow of Obedience makes me obey the order. I am amazed at how differently they and I have understood the Bible.

An opportunity to introduce our students to good cinema comes up. For me, films are a great medium to spread spirituality and religion among the youth today. The organizers of the Indian Film Festival of Thrissur 2006 (IFFT), headed by Cherian Joseph, are desperately hunting for an office from where they can function. This is a body of film-lovers, who organized a film festival with the support of the Corporation, the Mayor and the wealthy people of the town. They visit the college to meet a teacher to find out, and finally when they approach me, I suggest a room in the college quite convenient for the purpose. It is separate from any other rooms, has two doors and a veranda. My offer is taken seriously, and all of a sudden, I am informed that the Mayor is arriving the following day to inaugurate the Festival. Learning of this, I immediately inform the Vice- Principal and the seniors. They don't respond negatively, but I sense their disapproval. I turn to Jesus and plead: 'Jesus, let nothing unpleasant take place this month because of the office being here.' Jesus hears my prayers literally. Within a week, the sisters have been won over and are happy about the presence of the Film Festival office in the campus. One sister sitting up late in the college alone, says: 'I am not afraid to work till midnight. The presence of the brothers in the office wards off my fear.' Everything goes on smoothly and peacefully. Our students get a chance to gain exposure to different realities by viewing the movies—for free. The students who have free hours either in the morning or after lunch are allowed to go together and see the movies. I remind them, my daughters, that they are being sent only for the Festival. If they stray to any other place, they would be misusing their freedom, and this would invite curtailment of it; it would also mean that they are spoiling the chances for the next group of students to experience such a festival. I am proud of my students. How reliable and talented they are! When the university organizes 'The Fourth Estate Conference', the resource persons are amazed at the queries and observations of our students. 'Sister, they ask about serious films like *Page Three* and *Bicycle Thieves*. Very smart students!'

I get a call from a reporter of the *Vanitha* magazine for permission to interview the Film Club members in my college. I am thrilled and happily agree. These smart students will do it well, I know. They come and talk to my students in the hall as I am busy in the office. Later, I am called to the hall, just for a photograph with the students. While we are chatting, cracking jokes, and laughing, they click away. Before leaving, the journalists' team comes to the Principal's office to chat. I talk with them freely about many matters, but urge them to confine themselves to writing about my students. But when the issue comes out, it turns out to be a 'feature' about me. When a congratulatory e-mail comes from my student in Kuwait, I am terrified. I give the librarian strict instructions to bring the copy, when it comes to the college, directly to me. Without reading it fully, I ring up the Mother Provincial and ask for pardon and send her a copy. Next I rush to the Local Superior. I am relieved only when my Amma compliments me on the article. Very soon, the Mother Provincial pays an official visit and questions me on every sentence: 'Jesme, I'm convinced of what you say. But I'll have to answer the other sisters who question me.' When we are at the Generalate, the Mother General asks my batch mate about the article. She defends me and her words save me from trouble. When the Mother General asks me in an interview about the new horizons CMC should explore and develop, I suggest the field of media, especially film. She agrees with me but advises that only strong people like me can work in that field as it is 'slippery'.

I appreciate the CMI Congregation for having succeeded in starting four Chetanas by now, including the 'Film Chetana'. My argument is that if the Blessed Chavara, the Founder of both the CMI and the CMC, were alive, he would have asked us to wind up all the ordinary schools and colleges, for there are many agencies who work in the field now. Our main concern should be to set up media centres where we train the youth on how to critically assess the present media, how to create better media products and how to make it a viable means of propagating or instilling values. Whether we acknowledge it or not, the youth follow the media; instead of blaming them or moaning that the youth are being led astray, why not enter the field and do something serious and immediate to save the youth? In this venture, the Blessed Chavara will be proud of the CMI, but not yet the CMC.

In no time, I'm named a 'cine-nun' by many and I'm proud of the epithet. Films play a very important role in shaping the youth; and I appreciate the contribution of Lal Jose to society in producing such a striking film as *Achanurangatha Veedu*. It is based on the true story of a minor girl who falls prey to a pimp, and the hardships the whole family suffers as a result. The girl has two sisters—one, sent back after marriage because of dowry problems; another, whose marriage is fixed but is called off because of the youngest sister's situation. The family, except the youngest daughter, attempts to commit suicide by taking poisoned food. Ironically, when the family is arrested, the youngest one is once again taken away by the pimp. The film, *Kadhavasheshan* by T.V. Chandran, is for me one of the best films about the kind of compromises we make in our lives. A young man commits suicide. The girl whom he is to marry tries to find out the cause. She learns that he is a do-gooder, and after the gang-rape and murder of a girl whom he loved as his own sister, unable to cope with the injustice and cruelty of this world, he takes his own life. Along with such serious films, films with happy endings like *Chocolate* or *Niram*, about the merrymaking, misunderstandings, sacrifices, villainy, love and romance in college campuses, also contribute to values of the youth in a notable way.

In many of our prayer sessions when I'm asked to lead, I bring in themes from films. During Lent, I bring up the film, *The Passion of the Christ*, for discussion, with these remarks:

'The Jews object to the film saying it accuses them of Crucifixion; the Romans are against it, saying it pictures them as villains. But the director, Mel Gibson remarks: "To show that I am the cause for His Crucifixion, there is a special shot where my hand holding the nail to crucify Him is shown." Yes, each one of us is responsible for His Crucifixion; and also for the Crucifixion of many more Jesuses in our daily life.' I ask them what they think of the Crucifixion and its significance in their lives.

During the Mass, in the prayer of petition, I pray aloud: 'Jesus, *oru poo mathram chodichapol nee oru pookaalam thannu. Oru manalthari chodichapol nee kadaloram thannu. Ninte mahamanaskatha ulkollaan, ninnolam valaraan jnangale padipikoo.*' (Jesus, when asked for just one flower, you gave us the spring season; when asked for a grain of sand, you gave us the sea-shore. Teach us to imbibe your generosity and help us to grow up to you.) The following lines are sung to Jesus sleeping in the boat when the storm and the thunder frighten the disciples: '*Kaate nee veesharuthipol; kaarre nee peyyaruthipol; aaromal thoniyilente jeevante jeevaniripoo.*' (Let the wind not blow; let the black clouds not pour; the life of my life is in the beloved boat.) Gazing at the crucified Christ, one can sing: '*Oru kochu swapnathin chirakumaay aviduthe arikil jnan ipol vannenkil; oru noku kaanaan; oru vaaku kelkaan; orumicha dukhathil pankucheraan.*' (If only I could reach near you now, on the tiny wing of a dream—to get just a glimpse of you, to hear at least a word from you, and to partake in your suffering and grief.)

I have earlier mentioned a short film, *Vadakramam,* made by a young director, Kamal. This film becomes my theme for a prayer that I lead. The hero, a young man, feels his beloved sister who is blind, is a hindrance to his future life with his lady-love. He takes her to the railway track in the guise of 'showing' her a train, despite her request to go to the sea-shore. She is promised a visit to the beach after the 'sighting' of the train. Purposely, leaving her on the tracks, he stands nearby to witness the train going over and crushing her. The remains of her body are thrown into the sea. When the young man sits with his lady-love on the strand, pieces of his sister's dress are washed up on the shore by the waves. Unaware of the cruelty of her lover, the lady remarks: 'This beach smells like a graveyard.' He is seen sitting gloomy and frustrated. Can he ever find pleasure again, even though he has got rid of the obstacle in his life? Should we not accept such hindrances in life for the sake of ultimate peace? Such messages are presented before the sisters for meditation and thought, during the prayer time. Films and songs are discussed in terms of spirituality which, I think, is appreciated by the sisters. This is something which every religious person who is engaged with the youth today should pursue.

During 2007–08, which turns out to be my last year in the college, I feel we should do a campus film. My desire is that the story should come from the students. A talented teacher joins us from Amala College. We hunt for stories written by the students and published in our magazine. Two stories strike me, and the one pertaining more to women, *Thuruthile Pavizhaputtu* (Pearls in a Lonely Island), is selected. It is about the frequency of divorce these days; and it is also against the evil of abortion. A twist is introduced to the story in order to provide a happy and positive ending. A woman is standing outside a family court waiting for her divorce hearing to come up. She remembers that at the age of ten, she came here with her mother, who also underwent a divorce. Her quarrels with her husband are shown in a flashback. Now the girl is pregnant and she doesn't want her unborn child to meet the same fate, so she wants to abort. The lady doctor counsels her, and so she decides to give birth to the baby and to bring her up as an empowered woman, who will work for the good of society.

Finding a heroine becomes hard. Even in this day and age, many girls are not willing to act in a film, even of their own college. The first one selected refuses; the next one, too, replies in the negative. As I am a little crestfallen, a sister suggests I try the girl who wrote the story, since she has had stage experience. I am overjoyed; the girl agrees, telling her parents that she is acting in a documentary. The film needs a ten-year-old girl; the same girl, who was eight when she acted in *Jaalakangal*, is now of the age we need in the film. The film turns out to be a success. A brilliant student from our college gains experience and exposure as the associate director of the film. She bags the RANK award instituted by the *Malayala Manorama* daily and Air India, at the national level. The heroine gets the prize for the best actress in a short film competition.

Next comes the screening of campus and school-level films and the awards to the best films in both the categories. A team of dutiful and talented staff works hard, involving numerous students in the organizing and the conduct of the event. What a marvellous experience these students gain as a result. The event gets more media coverage than ever before. It turns out to be a process of 'spiritual and moral awareness' for the students as the films they make are free of the evils of commercialism, which promotes sex and violence; instead the students' films are guided by a positive value system for society. In general, such participation in extra-curricular activities fetches the college better results, even ranks, than before.

Unlike in my college, the film festival organized in another college screens films mostly around sexual themes. The 'virgin' students there watch the movies without any discussion or preparation. *Sancharan*, directed by a woman, is a beautiful film that depicts lesbianism with empathy. Such a film could be used to open up a discussion on the 'pairs' in colleges, especially hostels. This is also true for other films which are sometimes screened; without any discussion, such viewing would have the opposite effect, according to many of the students themselves, in this case, of encouraging lesbianism. I mention this problem during the valedictory address, when I am given a chance to evaluate the festival. But my considered comments get transformed into a rumour, spread by goodness-knows-who, that I am encouraging the screening of vulgar films in our college. Unnecessarily, I am targeted for severe negative criticism by the sisters. I remember the advice Fr Paul had received from Fr Gabrielle, about how to develop your talents even while remaining in the seminary or convent; he had shared this advice with me too, so I can carry on with my work.

My run-ins with the authorities at the college are nothing new. Even over the year-long celebration of the college Diamond

Jubilee, there is friction. The PTA and the Vice-Principal remind about this important event on the very day I take over. I am panic-stricken at their expectations of a grand celebration, as time is short. The inauguration is proposed for 1 July, at the height of the monsoons and college admissions. The commendable aspect of the function is the 'Gurupooja' when the senior-most in all the sections of the college—the Principals, the Managers, the chaplains, the local superiors, the superintendents, the PTA presidents, the staff and the students—are honoured. We offer them each a woollen shawl as a symbol of Mother Mary's shawl. Fortunately, Smt. Sugathakumari 'Teacher', the poetess, graciously consents to inaugurate the Jubilee, even though I have approached her by a mere telephone call. To my dismay, the first day of admissions falls on the same date as the inauguration. An alternative arrangement is to be made for the hall. The upstairs of the library is allotted for admissions with much difficulty. But the saddest part of it all is that the Manager absents herself from the function, stating a lame excuse. Later, the Provincial councillor for higher education, the former Principal of Amala, severely criticizes me, remarking that nowhere has she heard of Diamond Jubilee celebrations—that it is redundant and a waste of time and money. When the sisters learn about this, they are furious. One sister brings an old calendar of the neighbouring college, showing that they had invited the President of India for its Diamond Jubilee. This silences the sister-councillor for the time being. Meanwhile, the master plan for the year-long projects is submitted to the Manager and her council, and receives sanction. These projects comprise financial assistance to sixty deserving girls for their marriage, blood donation by sixty students, teaching handicrafts to the students as well as to deserving women, building a house for a deserving worker, and holding a series of lectures on the relevant topics of the day. Now comes the matter of fund-collection.

One morning, a woman enters my room with a request for a certificate, proving that she had been a student of this college. I immediately recognize her as Alice from the pre-degree batch in 1972–74. She is happy to learn that I'm Memy from the Arts group in that batch. I help to swiftly get the certificate issued to her. When she is informed of the Diamond Jubilee celebrations and the charitable deeds we are planning, she offers an amount of one lakh rupees.

For fund collection, the PTA suggests a 'Ganamela' led by the playback singer Rimy Tommy. But knowing about her high rates, we decide instead to book the 'Blind Orchestra' from Trivandrum. It becomes a very touching and heart-warming event. The PTA plans to bring the Governor, to inaugurate the valedictory function of the Jubilee celebrations. The Manager is displeased; she forgets that the President of India was the chief guest at the Diamond Jubilee celebrations of the neighbouring college. Anyway, finally, the Governor does not grace our function, as elections intervene and the college authorities cannot postpone the celebrations.

The next academic year begins with our week-long National Book Exhibition, in which more than twenty publishers participate. This becomes the first of its kind, as nowhere in south Kerala is this organized at the college level. Many interesting and colourful events like *Kaviyarangu* (poetry reading), magazine exhibition, tabla ensemble, and debates on current topics are arranged during the week. As Kerala is celebrating the golden jubilee of the state's formation, as part of the book display, an exhibition on different aspects of Kerala history is mounted in which all the departments set up stalls. This becomes the contribution of our students to the public. The entire student body gains through this process. The valedictory function of the National Book Exhibition is inaugurated by a roadside bookseller, Shamnaad, as I believe that the torch should be handed back to the one who organizes a display of books on the roadside, all 365 days of the year.

Twenty-five years of my professed life is over. Our batch of fourteen nuns celebrates our Silver Jubilee. For spiritual preparation, I should go to the Generalate at Aluva. While I am there, I am worried about the bursar's investment in a Life Insurance Scheme (LIS), which offers doubling of the investment. A few days later, I read in the papers about the LIS and the investments made in it. When I inform the bursar, she is unruffled because the Provincial councillor for higher education has also invested money in the LIS. I wonder at the worldliness and lack of prudence on the part of the senior sisters.

Something happens during my absence from the college for twenty-five days when I am in Aluva. The Superintendent has been collecting Rs 10,000 from those who reserve seats in the management quota for the self-financing courses. When they join, this amount is adjusted with their capitation fee. If they forsake the seat, the money will not be returned. Though I don't agree with this scheme of things, this has been the practice and I am bound to obey the management. No adjustments should be made without the Manager's consent. But when one woman pleads to the Superintendent to reserve the seat for Rs 5,000, she agrees as the woman promises to give the balance amount later. But then this woman starts demanding the money back. This is against the rules. It is a simple matter, but assumes ugly proportions. Summoning political support, she takes up the matter against us. Fearing things are getting out of control, after informing the Vice-Principal, I call the woman to request her to hand over the receipt to the Superintendent and get her money back. The woman screams and accuses me of shaking off the college's responsibility. All I can do is to repeat what I've told her. The next day, some boys, headed by a Calicut University senate member, come to see me. They know very well what I've told the woman, but they are out to get publicity for themselves. One of the boys waves the receipt at me: 'You are solely responsible for collecting this amount. Your signature is on the receipt.' When he hands it to me, I am puzzled. I have been away for twenty-five days, how can my signature be there? But I see that where the Principal has to sign, the Superintendent has signed without even marking, 'for' me. I prove the signature not to be mine, but I cannot help agreeing when they say that they did not know. They want me to call the Superintendent. I plead with them, 'Mon, why do you want to insult an elderly woman? Anyway, you are doing this to me. Isn't that enough?' I don't want to blame the Vice-Principal either for this discrepancy, though she was in charge when this happened. When I refuse to bring the Superintendent into the picture, the boys fly into a temper.

One of them opens the door, goes out, and brings his followers inside to shout slogans; they are accompanied by the police and TV crew. My security staff, attenders and the peon are stunned. The protesters demand I give my consent in writing, to which I repeat what I have already told the woman. Once they have taken photographs of the scene—which was what they really wanted to do in the first place—they retire without further harassment. I appreciate their fair dealing! The police come again enquiring if we have any complaint. I answer in the negative.

The Vice-Principal informs the Bishop, who requests not to mention his name or bring him into the picture. We are advised to get help from the Congress leaders. They regret the actions of the youth and sympathize with me and my associates. A member of the PTA, a well-wisher of the college, informs me that he will visit me. I am keen the Manager should meet him, but citing the example of the Bishop, she stays away. So much for the zeal of the Manager-cum-Provincial in a crisis! Instead of consoling me, she even tries to find fault. The PTA members come the next day. When the matter is explained to them, they express their desire to meet the Superintendent. But I dissuade them, unsuccessfully. The Superintendent refuses to come, on the plea that she is sick. I tell them not to compel her. But they are offended and protest that they have come here for the sake of the college, forsaking their work, because of the crisis created by her, and this is nothing but arrogance on her part. Pacifying them, I somehow wind up the meeting, thanking them for their prompt assistance. The Manager is angry when she learns of what the PTA had to say.

The strange part is that when the routine police verification after an unlawful assault, as the gherao is called, takes place, the Manager gets all flustered: 'Jesme, the police will come to the Principal's office, remove all the CDs from the shelves.'

'Why, Mother? What is the need for that?' I don't understand the connection. 'Jesme, if they find any pirated CDs, then that will create trouble.'

'Mother, not a single CD that I possess is pirated.' What does she think of me? What a mysterious mindset!

One day when the Manager enters the convent, she sees me at the door talking to the attender and her mother. As she passes by, she says, 'Jesme, I have to talk to you. Come to the Provincial House this evening.' I go to meet her without an inkling of the ordeal I am to face. Can people be so cruel? I am led to an interior room, which I see for the first time. Like a judge, she is seated on one end of the table, and she asks me to sit opposite her. In a triumphant tone, she starts reading from something which is hidden from my view. Such piercing accusations she reads out without flinching. Why doesn't she think of the 'wounded heart' sitting opposite her? This is what she reads: 'Sr Jesme, the Principal of St Maria's College, is constantly viewing "blue films" and forces the attender girls to view them. Besides, she indulges in sexual perversions with them. If she is not removed from the Principal's Chair, this matter will be published in the newspapers.' By a loyalist.

I don't know how I am sitting there! But at times of such crisis, a miraculous mental strength grips me. Wearing an artificial smile, I tell her, 'I know you won't believe the content of an anonymous letter. I assure you, that so far in my life, I have never laid a finger of mine with a wrong intention on any girl or boy.' The cross-examination continues in all seriousness. Looking as though she has thoroughly defeated me, she lobs this accusation: 'Have you asked any girl to remove her "top"?' I am confused. I have no memory of making such a comment. Have I ever told anyone so and in what context? When I ask her for a clue to my statement, she replies, 'It was heard long back.'

'Then why didn't you ask me then?'

'I waited for the right moment to come.' How can this trial be over? I strongly challenge her: 'You please come to the college and the convent and ask all of them. If a single person agrees with this letter as you suspect, I am ready to endure any punishment from you.' The Manager clarifies, 'A copy of this letter has been received by the Mother General. She wanted me to question you first.' I am broken-hearted. Tears brim over which, biting my lip, I try to suppress. How can she believe such terrible and mean things about me? More than the writer of the poison letter, I find it difficult to forgive the Provincial who, believing all this, questioned me. Being in position, I too get such anonymous letters. A letter abusing a hosteller's chastity comes to me and the warden. I tell the warden not to inform the girl about it; when such letters come repeatedly, I meet the girl's mother when she comes to the hostel to meet her daughter. I show her the letter, asking her to note the handwriting and find out the possible sender, and to be cautious. I don't lose confidence in the girl. When I receive a letter against a staff member, I tell her the content of it in the most caring way, assuring her that I don't believe a syllable of it. From the 'sharing box', I get many serious letters of accusation even against the warden, but I always console her.

Now, when a similar situation arises in my case, I am deeply distressed at how my authorities treat me. When I meet a reliable and mature attender girl, I ask her confidentially: 'Molé, do you remember any time hearing me ask anybody to remove her "top"?'

'Oh, Sister, has it reached you too?'

'Tell me. When did it occur?' And then she narrates the whole story: 'Don't you remember, Sister, the girl named A, poured a bucketful of water in a wash-basin which broke and fell on her ankle and crushed it? As this happened late in the evening and she had to go home the following day, you did not want her to climb the stairs to her room and so you made her sleep in the Council Room downstairs with the girl called B. After your work in the office, while returning to the convent at night, I was with you carrying your files. On the way, we went to the council room to check whether A's ankle had swollen. Then you saw her wearing tight churidar-pyjamas and a top, and you asked: "How can you sleep in so tight a dress? Shall we bring your nightie from your room?" She was reluctant to remove her pants, so you suggested that if she was wearing a petticoat, she might as well remove the top and sleep. So saying, we left the room. I carried your files up to the convent gate. Next day, I heard A complaining to C, her cousin, that you made her remove her top. C rushed to ask me what you had done and I assured her of the innocuousness of your words. But by the time A had shared it with her beloved sister, the whole convent knew about it, except you. I was a witness to it along with B who stayed with A that night. Even C believes in your innocence.' I don't know what the sisters think about it. I know A's beloved sister very well and why she is turning things against me. More proofs reveal the identity of the culprit. But the Provincial-cum-Manager visits the convent to question each sister to assess my character and the validity of the contents of the anonymous letter. Imagine the state of a Principal whose fate is to be decided by her subordinates. How much respect will they have left for her?

Whoever reports against the Principal is encouraged by the authorities. Only now I come to know of the daily phone calls from the Provincial's house to gather information about me. Given all this, it is a miracle that I am able to continue as Principal for almost three years. As the sisters are sure that I cannot be suspected of such behaviour, the Provincial decides not to punish me for the time being. When I am called for interview after she meets all the others, I lose my temper, as I am terribly upset. In anger, she dismisses me from her room. In the concluding meeting, she speaks well of the sisters who cooperated with her. Then she calls me to her side since she hasn't given me her 'blessings', as I was abruptly told to leave the room. I can't bear this charade any more and retort, 'I think, right now, I don't need your blessings, Mother. I will get it directly from Jesus for the time being.' The attempt to remove me from the chair fails utterly this time.

When I share my anguish about this letter with my staff and the attender girls, they are all ready to save me from this snare at any cost. If I am to be punished on the basis of an anonymous letter, I feel it is better that I quit the convent then and there itself; for the first time in my life, I think of leaving. I write an official letter to the Mother General requesting for a copy of that letter, and to personally meet her with the same plea. But she evades my request, consoling me to think of the agony of Jesus and to endure everything for the sake of everyone's good. As a meek and docile lamb, I return from the Generalate.

When the academic year 2007–2008 comes, someone inside me tells that this is my final year here. I start looking around the campus every morning, taking in and appreciating its beauty, the cool breeze, the Holy Grotto, the serene atmosphere, and much more. The Onam celebrations turn out to be jovial and enjoyable. One of the staff members comments, 'There has never been such a hearty Onam celebration here before, Sister.'

'That is because this is my final Onam here; that is why I have taken so much interest in making it lively.' Every time I discuss, do, or plan out things, I tell those around me: 'My mind says this is my final year here.'

'Have you got any signal to go to Amala College?'

'I haven't. This is my mind's whispering!'

Somebody asks the Vice-Principal: 'Sister, are you planning to take Sr Jesme away from here?'

'We haven't thought about it yet,' she replies.

But I am conscious about my every moment here. By November-end, the Sister-in-charge of sending Christmas greeting cards asks me to write a Christmas message to be printed with my signature underneath. I suggest to her to print a few more cards than last year, when she says: 'Sister, it will be wasted because it can't be used next year, as you won't be here.'

'Who told you that I won't be here?'

'Sorry, Sister, you always say so.' She is embarrassed when everybody pokes fun at her.

As Principal, I have seen several highs and lows. The students' enthusiasm, especially in organizing and participating in extra-curricular activities, in film festivals and so on, have given me great joy. So also the concern and loyalty of some of the sisters, attenders and PTA members. But equally, I have had to face accusations, often imaginary, of the authorities—of showing the youth vulgar films; of giving them too much freedom; being troublesome, when I point out administrative and financial irregularities in the college; and plainly of being too outspoken, a veritable crime where the Vow of Obedience reigns supreme; or maybe of going too fast in providing the students with exposure, much to the discomfort of the majority of the sisters. The new battleground will be my health.

The Mother Provincial visits the college to tell me that she has come across a sister-doctor, a dermatologist-cum-neurologist, who is the councillor of another Province. She, along with the Mother General, has talked to this doctor about me. The Provincial wants me to consult this doctor for my hypothyroid and for the discoloration of the skin on my forehead. I became a thyroid patient in 1997, over eleven years back. She offers to accompany me to the doctor. Quite innocently, I respond: 'Mother, how can you, who has more important duties to perform than this, find time to take me that far? You need not come, Mother. I will go with the other sisters.' She insists, 'No, Jesme. It is my pleasure to take you.'

The following day, she rings up and tells me that she will

send the car of the Provincial to pick me; I am to be accompanied by a Provincial councillor, who is of my batch, and a sister, who is my spiritual friend. I suggest to her that I would prefer Amma, or somebody from home, to come with me. Fortunately, she agrees. Amma and my youngest sister accompany me and I meet the sister-doctor after many hours of waiting. The discussion is about my life as a whole, not just my medical history, and finally we come to the topic of my thyroid problem. 'Jesme, what medicine are you taking for thyroid?'

'Thyroxine. If it is not available, I get Eltroxine.'

'Tell me exactly which. One is for a different illness than the other.'

'The pharmacist tells me that they are interchangeable.'

'Never. Your skin colour change maybe due to psoriasis.'

'If Jesus so desires, I will have to endure it.'

'Jesme, you don't know the seriousness of it. The whole skin will ooze pus and the foul smell will keep people away from you.'

'If Jesus blesses me with that, should I not accept it, Sister?'

She wants my blood to be examined. I tell her that I will do it at the polyclinic in Thrissur. But she wants me to do it in her hospital itself. It is already dark, but we are taken to her hospital and my blood sample is taken. Now she checks my pressure and loudly exclaims, 'Oh! See the pressure! It is all because of your tension.' She shows the reading to my batch mate who is also a nurse. I have checked my blood pressure quite often and have always found it more or less normal. On the way back to the convent, in the car, I ask my batch mate: 'Is there any serious problem in my pressure reading?'

'Only minor variations, Jesme. Usually, doctors don't bother about them.' So my doubts are justified. 'I have lost faith in that sister. What a hullabaloo she created after checking my pressure? That time itself, I felt that she was not being genuine.'

'Jesme, if you don't trust her, you should yourself have a thorough check-up at the polyclinic,' suggests my spiritual friend. God is speaking through her. I am relieved as that is a good solution.

The following day, soon after Mass, I go to a doctor nearby with an attender-sister. He examines my blood pressure and advises me: 'Sister, just avoid pickles for a month. You don't need any medicine.' I get a note from him, prescribing tests for thyroid, diabetes and cholesterol, and also asking me to do an ECG. Accompanied by the Assistant Mother, I go to the polyclinic and get all the tests done. In the evening, when I show the doctor the results, he gives me a clean chit. I come back to the convent elated and immediately share everything with the Local Superior, saying that I only need to continue my tablets for hypothyroid. 'Praise the Lord!' says the sister standing near the Superior.

Reaching the college, I am going through files, when I get a phone call from the sister-doctor: 'Jesme, your results have come. You have low HB (haemoglobin).'

'Usually, it is only that much, Sister.'

'You have to reduce the dose of your medicine for thyroid.'

'Sister, my doctor told me to continue it.'

'No, Jesme. Your doctor is misleading you. Besides, you have cholesterol. The treatment is to be begun soon. You should immediately come here for treatment.'

'Sister, I don't have cholesterol.' She goes on repeating all this and I keep rejecting her diagnosis.

I want to now consult a third doctor to know the exact condition. Soon, I get the Local Superior's consent to go to a thyroid specialist in Ernakulam, in the college minibus, with a sister and our own driver. The doctor examines the results and tells me to continue the same dose for three more months. When I seek to clarify whether there is any difference between Thyroxine and Eltroxine tablets, which the chemist gave me later, he assures me they are the same. 'But a sister-doctor, who is a specialist, tells me that they are different.'

'If everyone knew all the truths, we would have become Gods, Sister,' he says jocularly. 'Wait for three more months and then I will permit you to reduce the dose a little.'

Relaxed, I return and happily share the doctor's diagnosis with the sister and driver. A phone call comes from the Provincial, to tell me that the sister-doctor thinks it is time to begin my treatment. 'Why don't you go to her hospital at the earliest?'

'Mother, I don't need the treatment. I'm perfectly okay.'

'She told me you are suffering from cholesterol.' I update her on the results from the polyclinic and what the endocrinologist, whom I've just consulted, says. Unconvinced, she harps on, 'Even if you think you don't have cholesterol, what is wrong in being treated for it?' I cannot contain myself any more and burst out, 'Oh, Mother! What do you mean? My Amma won't say so.' The Provincial did not expect this, so she retreats, saying, 'Jesme, I think you are in the bus. People might hear. I'm hanging up.'

The driver and the sister accompanying me are unhappy. From my replies, they have understood that something's the matter. They can only sympathize with me. I feel so upset. What is in the minds of my authorities? They are very secretive and cunning. Do they think that I am lying about my test results? Reaching the convent, I send a copy of the tests results to the Provincial and the councillors to convince them. What else can I do?

So far, the Superior of the convent is very understanding and motherly. She consoles me during the crisis at the college, lovingly finds me free time for the Local Council meetings, encourages me to lead the group prayer in the convent and appreciates my spontaneous prayer during the daily Mass. She appreciates my offer to absorb into the college office an elderly and difficult sister who is to be relieved of her hostel duties. I remind the sisters who disagree with my decision, that old age will overtake us all one day.

When the term of three years is over, the Superior is transferred to a neighbouring convent. I am supposed to attend a seminar in Bangalore on the day she leaves, but I cancel my trip when she expresses the desire that I should be there on the day of her departure. Being the Second Councillor in the convent, it becomes part of my duty too.

The one who takes charge as Superior had been formerly our Superintendent. She knows me very well. I thank my Vice-Principal, Sr Meslin, who is also the Provincial Councillor for selecting this sister to be our Superior. But the breeze turns into a storm against me. She doesn't get involved in any of the serious affairs of the college. The authorities expect me to discuss everything that happens in the college with my Superior. She does not want to lose her peace of mind, so she keeps away from troubles. As no help can be expected from her, I solve the problems on my own. Gradually, I come to realize that she dislikes me. I can inform the Provincial about the Superior's attitude, but I refrain. I have suffered much by others reporting against me to the authorities and don't want to do the same, though now I am in a position to do so; such lack of action on my part is interpreted as a defect and I am aware of it. My friends tell me to inform the Provincial about the matter, as the authorities will usually favour the 'first reporters'—only with prejudice, do they listen to those coming later. But I hate doing this. So I am always either the 'second' or the last to talk about these happenings.

I rarely remember dates and numbers. But I can never forget 6 December 2007, not only because it is the anniversary of the destruction of Babri Masjid, but also because that day highlighted my tragedy as a nun and a Principal. There are two occasions that day when I get really angry. I am struggling to manage the college and the hostel with fewer sisters, when the warden of the 'plus two' hostellers (our hostel provides accommodation for various students, including to the plus two students of the Sacred Hearts school) decides, without telling me, to attend a course arranged by the Provincialate. The chief warden and the assistant warden are busy with official matters regarding a serious problem in the hostel. The servants assisting the cheduthies in the hostel kitchen are not paid properly, and this has come to the notice of the labour department. If the warden for the plus two students too absents herself for some days, the hostellers will be without any 'shepherd'. I explain the situation to the warden concerned, after discussing with the other wardens, and request her not to go. But the following morning, the Local Superior tells me that the Provincial Council has ordered the warden to attend the course, even if the Principal objects to it. I am angry because of the lack of understanding on the part of the authorities.

Soon another incident adds to my irritation. When the college opens, I come to know from the students that an additional amount of money is being collected from each one of them without proper sanction from me, ostensibly for photocopying their original documents. The students are ready to provide copies of their originals, but the sisters want to collect money and photocopy every document. The sight of the original documents lying in the photocopying room annoys me. When confronted, the sisters lie and put the blame unnecessarily on the students. My policy is that the college exists for the sake of the students. They are the pivot of the institution. We often forget that the Principal, the Vice-Principal, the teaching and the non-teaching staff exist in the college only because there are students. When I share these thoughts with the sisters or teachers, they are unable to accept them.

That day, minutes after this incident between the sisters and the students, I happen to see the Mother General stealthily walking into the college with a bag under her arm. She does not bring the vehicle inside the compound, but leaves it outside, in order to come in quietly and catch us unawares. She is embarrassed when I notice the manner of her entry. All the sisters come running; we all have lunch together and it is a jovial atmosphere. After lunch, the General calls me for a 'personal interview'. Someone informs me that she has been summoned by the Local Superior, who is her batch mate, for this interview, and that she has been informing the General of every movement of mine.

The General seems to be under some pressure to mete out punishment to me. She is saintly and politely tells me.

'Jesme, I have come here to remove you from the chair of the Principal.' Shocked, but hiding my feelings, I ask her: 'Mother, will you remove me from the nunnery also?'

'If you prefer so, that too can be done.'

'I would like to know the reason.'

'There are complaints against you from the staff about your hot temper.'

'I don't believe they will complain, Mother. They all love me.'

'That's your false impression,' she adds sneeringly.

'Mother, what is my fault? I think I have the right to know.'

'I can't speak it with my mouth. You speak of "sex".'

'Mother, what do you mean? Please be specific. Give me an example.'

'I cannot explain that. Anyhow, I want to take you to Aluva and make you translate many articles.' I look at Jesus inside me. He shows me the sign of victory. I don't understand what He says but I trust in Him. Suddenly, a sister dashes into the room to announce that our main generator has exploded all of a sudden. The workers are trying to extinguish the fire. 'Jesme, do you want to go and see?'

'No, Mother. My workers will do the needful. Let us continue this trial.'

'Jesme, the present Pope says that one out of every ten nuns is mentally disturbed and needs treatment. My plan is to take you to a doctor and get you some medicine.'

'Mother, I don't want any medicine. This has been tried by Mother Claudia ten years ago. Are you going to do the same to me?'

'I don't want to know what happened before. I was not the General then.'

'You talked to the sister-doctor at Palai about me, the Provincial said. Was the attempt to treat me there, a part of this treatment?'

'I never talked to her about you. It is a deed of foolishness on the part of the Provincial.'

Without consenting to the treatment, I come away. She wants to interview every sister to gather news about me. Meanwhile, I call Amma informing her about the General's command that I should undergo a 'mental treatment'. Amma tells me to bring the Mother General home to meet her.

While the General's interview of the other sisters is going on, I go to the college to check on the burnt generator. I ask my Vice-Principal-cum-Provincial Councillor: 'With Mother General enquiring about me from the sisters, how will they continue to respect me as their Principal? Won't they consider me as an *oochali*, a worthless creature?'

'The term you just used is disgusting. This is why the Mother General says that you use vulgar words.'

'This is a colloquial word, Meslin. How can it be vulgar?'

She is silenced. Then the hostel warden tells me: 'You spoke linking the administrator, a male, to a female guest lecturer. That is what the General meant by the word "sex", when she confronted you.'

'Disobeying me twice, the "guest faculty" gave the collected money to him. Naturally, I questioned it.' She doesn't say anything more.

By evening, the interviews are over. Now the Mother General calls me to her side and tells that she has made arrangements with the Local Superior to take me to a doctor. I plead with her not to send me, but she narrates an incident involving another sister. She had been reluctant to undergo treatment, but finally she agreed, and now she is very happy—she even goes around telling everybody how effective and soothing is the medicine. The General continues: 'When you start the treatment, you should take long leave.'

'If it is so soothing, why do I need to take leave, Mother?'

'In the initial stages, the treatment can be very disturbing and upsetting. Only after a period, the soothing effect sets in.'

I tell her, 'Mother, I have talked about this to my Amma. She wants to meet both of us.'

'In that case, let us take a sister with us, so that you can return with her after the visit.'

'Why can't I stay tonight with my Amma?'

'Haven't you already stayed home one day, this year?'

'No, I haven't.'

'Then, let me inform the Superior about it.' A new rule has been passed by the CMC authorities by which we are allowed to spend one day and night at home in a year. That night, we reach home and the General talks to Amma confidentially. Amma requests for one month's time to take me to a doctor herself and then see. The General is persuaded to agree as it is a genuine request. That night I spend with my Amma, after a long gap.

That Friday happens to be the first of the month, noted for the prayer and Mass at a church dedicated to the Sacred Heart of Jesus. Amma used to call me to attend the prayer there, but I have not been able to so far. She is happy that Jesus has brought me here on this day. We go to the church and spend the whole day in prayer. She doesn't want to send me back to the convent, after learning about their attempts at my treatment. I desperately want to go to Kurissupalli in Calicut, where the prayer on Friday is supposed to be very powerful. To reach there on the same day, I take a bus after informing the Local Superior that I am going to Calicut for prayer and to get some peace, and will return only after a few days. I used to go there in times of trouble even before, and the sisters know about it. But this Superior is unlike others and is hunting for my failures and weaknesses.

A few teachers in the college dare to help me and take me into confidence. A sister also takes a great risk in supporting me. She argues in favour of me with many in the college and the convent; she goes to the Mother General requesting her to reconsider her decision against me, and even writes a letter about me addressed to Mother. Before posting, she gives me the letter—she uses an inland letter form so that I won't be able to tear it up—for reading and despite my pleas, she goes ahead and drops it in the post-box. A senior member of the staff informs me that a 'guest faculty' with some grievance against me has been sent to the Manager by the Vice-Principal, in order to force her into writing a complaint, which can be filed as proof against me. The guest faculty had insulted me in the presence of TV people and senior staff. But later, we became friends and hence she is repentant that she had to give in to coercion.

The constant reference to the medication for mental treatment frightens me. When I come to the refectory, if anything is kept on my plate at the dining table, I won't have it for fear of drugs. Setting it aside, I take food only from the common table. Most of the time, I get food from the hostel kitchen, cooked by Mariamkutty Cheduthi and her assistant Celina Cheduthi. Till the very last day in the convent, these two are my intimate friends. How much they love me, serve me, pray for me, and suffer for my sake, I can't describe.

Amma is pestered by frequent phone calls from the Mother General asking about my treatment. We had asked her for one month's time, but these repeated calls are quite disturbing for a widow of seventy-two. One day, Amma takes me to a homeopathic doctor, to consult him about my thyroid problems. He promises to prepare the medicine and give it after two days. But I don't go to him again, as I know that I don't need it because I'm already taking Eltroxine tablets.

The serious complaint of the sisters is that I don't attend the Mass offered at the convent chapel in the morning. This is because I cannot get up in the mornings due to my hypothyroid problem. So I go to one of the neighbouring churches and attend the Mass in the evening. The sisters inform the authorities or spread the false rumour that I don't attend Mass at all.

One day, my youngest brother suggests that I consult Fr Panakkal of Potta Ashram for my problems. I go there with Amma and my sister-in-law. When my predicament is explained, he responds: 'Sister, Jesus doesn't want you to leave your chair. You are there by His divine plan. You shouldn't quit the post; besides, none will be able to dismiss you.' We talk about the problems over the self-financing courses and my attitude against the Church's decisions regarding them. But I also add that I have never acted against the pronouncements of the Church, bound as I am by the Vow of Obedience. His reply is striking: 'It is not when robbers enter a house that its members should go about reforming themselves. Let us together fight against the enemies; then we can criticize or reform ourselves.' I ask him for further guidance and he suggests, 'You may go to the Bishop and explain matters to him. He may get angry but you should endure it and tell him everything. Assure him that you are with the Church. When you have holidays, come here and pray.' I am much relieved and at peace. Sharing everything with Amma, I ring up my brother and reveal my happiness.

Reaching the convent, the sisters ask me about the meeting with Fr Panakkal. I try to fix an appointment with the Bishop. He tells me to call after two days. The second time, he asks: 'Principal, what happened? Isn't Jesus near you?'

'Jesus is very well near me. But certain things, we have to share with authorities, who are human.' He is too busy to meet me and so he puts me on to another father. I don't see the point of sharing my difficulties with anyone else than the Bishop and so don't go.

As advised by Fr Panakkal, I go to the Divine Retreat centre on a Sunday and spend the whole day in the presence of the Blessed Sacrament. With a great feeling of solace, I return to the convent. Accompanied by the hostel wardens and kitchen maids, I am to go on a trip to the Shrine of Velankanni Matha, the day after Christmas. With a heavy heart, I am about to leave, when the two Provincial councillors come in to tell me that all my trials are over; the file against me is closed and I can continue being the Principal. Overjoyed, I inform the wardens and immediately ring up Amma to give her the happy news, and ask her to tell everybody to thank Jesus in my name.

At Velankanni, I sit for a long time in the presence of the Blessed Sacrament, thanking Jesus and telling Him that I have reached the pinnacle of my suffering and can endure no more. Returning to the convent, I ask Jesus whether to share everything with my sisters or not. Getting His blessings, I tell the Superior that I have something to tell the sisters in general during the recreation time. With her permission, I tell them why I had been gloomy and silent all these days, and add that the file against me has been closed and I have been asked to continue as Principal. 'I ask your pardon for how I have behaved in the past few weeks. For anything you have done to me, I forgive.'

Getting permission from the Superior, I go to sleep early because I am exhausted from the trip. But as I slip into sleep, I am informed that I have a phone call from the Mother General. I promise to call back the next day. But even before I can call, the General calls and starts scolding me: 'You are to go to the Divine Retreat centre tomorrow itself and attend the Retreat there. But before you go, you are to take a "long leave". When the next term begins, you should not be on the chair. I have arranged everything regarding your meeting a doctor and taking medicine. We met Fr Panakkal and he told us that what you told is a lie. He allowed us to remove you from the chair. Your mother and brothers have already agreed to take you to a doctor and give you medicine. Now your family won't support you. Your brothers told me to do anything that would save you from the present predicament. I am about to go to Mangalore within an hour and will return only on the third of January. Then you are to call me for getting further instructions.'

How this twist of events has occurred, I wonder. Later, I learn of the phone calls from the Superior to some people after I had gone to sleep. I realize that I am at the end of my tether. Tearfully, I call Amma, who tells me, 'Molé, what she said is a big lie. I am at Mattam attending the death ceremony of my brother. She called here and told me that your sons have agreed to treat Jesme. And she wanted me to give my permission. I told her, "I don't believe that my sons have told you this. Let me talk to them." When I asked them, they assured me that they hadn't said anything of the sort. Joshy's wife is shaking with anger hearing the lie told by the Mother General.'

I know that there are only hours left for me to escape. Tomorrow, I have to go for the Retreat. At the Divine Retreat centre, any type of drug can be forced upon me, as I know what my chechie suffered there years back. I won't be able to escape from the advances of the 'brothers' there. It is then that I remember a friend of mine with whom I had jokingly shared this event of being removed from the chair, and the drama around the medication to be administered to me. I call him and inform about the situation. He advises me to hear what one of his friends has to say. The friend calls and tells me of the ways and means by which I can protect myself. Sara Joseph, the acclaimed Malayalam writer and feminist-activist, offers her assistance. But I tell my friend to talk to my brother and give him his phone number. After a while my brother comes to meet me, listens from the horse's mouth and asks me to get ready by 3 p.m., if I am planning to go home. I give my consent, take my original documents, bid farewell to Virgin Mary, the Mother of Jesus at the Grotto, and leave the college 'holding' the hands of Jesus. The sisters are on leave attending the Annual Recollection Prayer from which I am spared as I am to attend the five days' Retreat at the Divine centre. Through the intercom, I inform the Superior that I am going home with my brother on an urgent errand. That is my first attempt to escape from the Formidable Fortress.

5

THE SAFE ANCHORAGE

Before I reach home, Amma is brought back from her brother's place at Mattam. I get home emotionally upset, thinking of the worst that can happen. My Amma, brothers and sister-in-law welcome and console me. The only clothes I have is the dress I'm wearing. But my brother tells me that I should remain in the habit and always be near Amma. Every night, I wash my dress and spread it under the fan to dry. Meanwhile, I don't meet anybody except my family members.

My greatest grief during these days is the negative attitude of one of my sibling sisters. While working in the college, the nuns, especially the Superior, have brainwashed her by showing special affection. The Superior and her Assistant come home, but I remain in my room. My brother wants me to just come in and see them; or else, they will think that I am not there. As the Mother General is in Mangalore, any decision to be taken about my case will only be after her return.

On 1 January is my Feast day, as it is believed that Jesus was named on that day. It is normally celebrated in the college by the students, staff, PTA, and the sisters. But this time, I can't even attend the Mass as I am in hiding. On 3 January is the Feast of the CMC and CMI Founder, the Blessed Chavara Kuriakose Elias. Every year, my sister celebrates this feast at the church at Ollur. I go to Ollur for the Mass with Amma; and just behind me is my batch mate, but Amma saves me from being spotted by her. That day, I visit my father's grave and get his blessings to leave CMC; and then I pray to Anumol, my dead seven-month-old niece, to give me strength to quit CMC; and after that, I pray to my late chechie, seeking her blessings for success. Then I bid farewell to the Blessed Chavara who I love and admire very much. The Bible messages also give me signal to leave. I have a gift for feeling such signals. On so many occasions have I opened a page of the Bible after prayer and found lines which would be prescient of the happenings of that day. Amma says that she will not send me back to such a 'hell'.

Meanwhile, a priest is brought as a mediator, and he suggests that I go to 'Kurishumala' and spend a year in prayer. I readily agree to this and my brother wants me to meet the Senior Bishop and get his blessings for this period of prayer. At the appointed time, Amma and I go to him. While sharing my recent bitter experiences, I start weeping. I ask his permission to go to 'Kurishumala'. He replies: 'Jesme, you won't understand whether you are mentally disturbed or not. Only the other sisters will know it. So this is not the time to go for prayer. As soon as you can, see a doctor and start the treatment.' He doesn't listen to Amma nor even look at her. Amma is very upset after the meeting as she expected a little more kindness and concern from the Bishop.

When the Mother General comes back to the Provincial house from Mangalore, my brother is invited for a discussion. He makes them promise never to give me 'medication' under any circumstances. They assure him that they will take me back, forgiving me unconditionally. I plead with Amma never to send me back to the convent and she agrees. If I am sent back, I confess, I will run away while being taken to the Generalate. If that is not possible, I may put an end to my life. At this, one of my family members callously responds, 'It would be far better if you elope with someone; or that someone is ready to marry you. Then we will not have your burden. Even if you commit suicide, it will be better than your entering our set-up. For a while we may suffer; after a while we will forget.'

Even though Amma strongly objects to these statements, I get an idea of the general attitude of the family. Next day, I am taken to the Provincial house along with Amma, my brother, sister-in-law, and my uncle's son. Two of my friends, Asha and Smitha, insist upon being there, as representatives of civil society. They will be with me just for moral support. Only if I am willing one hundred per cent, will they allow me to go back to the convent. As I meet the Mother General, she embraces me and denies whatever she has said over the phone. I can't understand why she does so. Then I am brought to the room of the Provincial who also welcomes me back with a hug. It is a moving scene where everyone, including me, is weeping. My Amma and all the family return while I am taken back to the college by the two councillors and made to take the Principal's chair. I had asked for a month's time, to go for personal prayer, to which they agreed.

I get a very warm welcome from my sisters, students and teachers except one newly appointed teacher who has worked against me. One sister, who I suspect to be the hand behind the 'anonymous letter', has undergone a tremendous transformation. She is very friendly towards me. The two cheduthies, Mariamkutty Cheduthi and Celina Cheduthi in the hostel kitchen, who are almost like my Amma, receive me back with even more love. But the Local Superior is not much impressed by my return, even though like a top actress, her behaviour is pleasant. My preference of places for prayer is rejected one after the other. It is cold in Kurishumala and Sameeksha, as they are up in Kalady, and hence I am not allowed to go there. At last, they agree to Sameeksha, but I get permission to stay there only for a week. I wish to take leave for only that long, but the Provincial compels me to take one month's leave. The College Day has been fixed for that month, and if I am on leave, it will be held in my absence. I have never heard of a College Day being conducted in the absence of the Principal. The Provincial's demand reveals her ulterior motive. My brother recognizes the trick but pleads with me to obey. I tell him: 'You saved me from the tigers and brought me back to the same den.'

I take one month's leave and go to Sameeksha, an ashram for quiet prayer run by the SJ Fathers. There, the CMC authorities arrange a sister's brother, who is a priest, to counsel me. When I share my experiences, he is scared to guide me as he suspects my involvement in party politics. Thus, I escape the wiliness of the authorities who have arranged a counsellor of their choice to guide me. While at Sameeksha, I get a phone call from a college teacher asking if I am undergoing treatment at a mental hospital, as they have been informed by Principal. Another one tells me about his friend's remark that I am undergoing treatment for mental illness. Who is spreading this rumour? Not my friends or family members; it is being spread by only those who stand to benefit from such news.

Reaching the prayer house, I spend three whole days in the chapel where the Blessed Sacrament, exposed inside the tabernacle, is visible through the glass door. I don't utter a single prayer to Him. Instead, I silently gaze at Him, with only one request: 'Speak to me directly. Now, I will believe only Your words.' Nothing happens for three days, but in the evening of the third day, He opens His eyes, parts His lips and speaks. 'Why do you say you had been in the convent for twenty-six years? Count and see how many years have passed after you left home for CMC.' I count and am puzzled at the number thirty-three. These are the number of years that Jesus spent on earth.

'Jesme, your life in the CMC is over. So far, you have been undergoing only "desert experiences". Now you are going through the "death experience" at the same age as I did. You are dying for the CMC. Don't blame anybody. I'm doing it through them.'

'Jesus, what am I to do?'

'Before the thirty-fourth year, you will leave CMC. You will have a new life from then on.'

'Jesus, where? When? How?'

'Jesme, you are to lead the lay-religious.'

'Lord! Why do you talk paradoxically?'

'There are many who need your help.'

I sit for hours in His presence; He gives me assurance and mental strength. I don't know the details of my mission. But, from that moment onwards my prayer becomes, 'Jesus, show me Your way! Sacred Heart of Jesus, I place my trust in You.' I am relieved that He has spoken to me. Those who say that I am insane will certainly think that this is part of my madness. But Jesus will prove His words in the course of time. I have nowhere to go after ten days at Sameeksha. My friend and sister inform me of a Retreat on the other side of the river, beside which I stay. While in prayer, I remember my cousin, Fr Joseph, who is transferred to Delhi from Hyderabad. 'He can help me,' my mind tells me. I consult Amma and she agrees. So my next concern is to get his number. The number had been saved in my mobile when I had gone to Hyderabad on a tour. Fortunately, I find it and send a message to him that 'I am in trouble'. After an hour of waiting, he calls me. I describe my plight and that I want to have a consultation with him regarding my future. He is free only in the last week of January. 'I can be there then, Father.'

The next difficult step is to get permission from both the Mother General and the Provincial. I seek the help of Jesus, 'If You want me to go there, help me.' I call my friend Linux to reserve a ticket from Ernakulam to Delhi. If I don't get the permission, it can be cancelled. Gathering mental strength, I call the Mother General who consents to the idea, but only on the condition that the Provincial agrees. Then I call the

Provincial, ask the Father to call both the Provincial and the General, and after many phone calls and explanations, the sanction is received. The Provincial sends her car along with two sisters to take me to the railway station. I spend eleven days in Delhi during the coldest days of the year. The first day itself I meet the Principal from my neighbourhood, who propagated that I am undergoing mental treatment. She has also been spreading the same message in the place where I stay.

Those days, I share everything with the Father, including what Jesus had told me. But he doesn't believe this and advises me not to take a harsh decision all of a sudden. Instead, he proposes to me to avail two years' leave, in order to serve in the youth ministry with him. The General and the Provincial agree to grant me leave, something which they have been ready to do for a long while.

Coming back to the college, I place a request with the Provincial who gets the consent of her Council and forwards it to the Mother General for approval. On receiving the official permission in writing, I prepare to apply for 'long leave'. It is Lent and, naturally, I think of taking leave at the end of March, that is, after Easter. But I get a phone call from the Provincial, asking me to take leave immediately. I literally break down, and go home to tell Amma. My nephew comes and consoles me: 'Auntie, why do you stick on, if they don't want you to stay? You have stopped the donations and the capitation fee. They don't want such a Principal here. The church is after money and power that goes with being one. They might need to reintroduce the capitation fee at the earliest. For that, you should be away. Understand the situation and leave the place with joy.' I feel boosted. When I share this latest development with the father at Delhi, he consoles me and urges me not to stay on. He will try his level best to find accommodation for me.

To meet the Provincial in person, I go to the Provincialate. But she meets me only in the company of all the councillors. I relay my decision to go to Delhi within a week. Coolly, she says, 'Jesme, only because you ask for it, I allow you to go now.' What a paradox! Anyway, I immediately respond: 'Mother, I was not willing. But you revealed your desire that I should go now. Like Jesus in the Gethsemane, I pray for the strength to say: "Let this chalice pass me; but it is not my will but Thy Will be done."' She defends herself, 'Jesme, I only wanted you to take leave soon. I didn't want you to leave for Delhi before Easter.' I express my surprise at this remark. Surely, she did not want me to sit in a corner of the convent until Easter, after taking leave? I turn to the Provincial, saying that Easter is everywhere and it can be celebrated in Delhi too. But I am sad that I couldn't celebrate my Feast on New Year's Day in the company of my students, staff and sisters. Also, I regret that I could not organize my College Day and be with my dear ones on that day.

'It is sad that you are going away. It all happened so, Jesme,' says the Provincial. Finally, before taking leave, I say, 'As in the Bible, it is good that I am going away; I will send the "paraclete" to you all. I feel that "the same hands which delivered me have smothered me to death". I hesitate to ask why you made me a Principal at all, if you had planned to bring me down? I recognize it to be God's Plan.' All of them come to the auto which takes me to my place. I add: 'All the councillors and the Provincial are related to me, one way or the other. The Provincial is my brother-in-law's dear one; the Assistant Provincial is my teacher and friend; the Councillor for Higher Education is my own Vice-Principal; the Councillor for School Administration is my confidante; the one for the Hospital Administration is just senior to me in my batch; and the next one had been my friend. How ironic that in such an atmosphere the worst thing should happen to me!' My Vice-Principal tells me: 'Bless me, Jesme!' I hear it the other way around as: 'Don't curse me.' For, the guilt feeling, similar to that of Judas', might have prompted her to utter those words. But I have only blessings for them all! 'Jesus, they know not what they do; forgive them!'

Before my leaving, another problem crops up—they want to bring the next Principal to the college before I go. In a normal situation, I would be ready to welcome my successor. But given all this rejection and bitterness, I am not in a mood to entertain the idea. Amma advises me to go and sit in Dolour's Church if that happens. The father in Delhi tells me to stay at home.

My student-sister and my batch mate lovingly help me pack my luggage. I have to come back at the end of March, as my signatures are required on many of the files and documents. Why I should leave three weeks ahead of the end of March is the genuine question of all who love me. My student-sister reserves three-tier AC tickets to and from Delhi, out of much concern. The father at Delhi offers to pay the rent and the mess fee for my service—not more, nor less.

The *Gruhalakshmi* magazine, through Prof. Kusumam,

informs me of a district award as recognition for my work in the field of education, along with four others in various fields. The press want to meet me about this. The Provincial seems scared about this meeting, as she reminds me not to utter a word to them about the ordeal I have undergone these recent months. All these four months, my two friends at the media who know my story in detail, have saved me from publicity. When I plead with my authorities not to dismiss me from the post all of a sudden, lest the media get wind of it, they sneer at me. They think that I am boasting out of foolishness and pride. During the Award ceremony, I speak very positively and announce my decision to leave Kerala for two years in order to work in the youth ministry. One of the leaders sitting beside me says: 'Sister, the sisters may not need you here. But we need you. So come back soon.' I feel touched by a finer emotion.

The journey to Delhi is pleasant and safe. Fr Joseph cannot meet me at the platform as platform tickets are not being issued due to a bomb threat. A CBI official and a retired government official, who are my co-passengers, help me carry my heavy luggage outside where the father waits for me with a car. He tells about his difficulty in finding accommodation for me at short notice. 'Jesme, I thought of making you stay at our Provincial house until I get another place. But someone has spread false notions about you. The Rector tells me that he has confidentially heard something against you and confessed his unwillingness to accommodate you here.' Can rumour and false accusations have so grave an impact on innocent 'people? Finally, Fr Joseph takes me to a nursing sisters' hostel where I stay in a posh room with all the amenities.

For three months, I am without any work. Till noon, I sit in my room and weep or reflect or stare at the ceiling. If I am seen around, the sisters there might suspect that I don't have a job. A Principal taking leave for two years and simply sitting in Delhi arouses curiosity. After lunch, I go to the chapel and spend time in prayer and adoration. This is the time when I look at Jesus and pray to Him to show me His way. I lack the courage to do what He has revealed to me. If it is His Will, let Him take the lead. Meanwhile, I go to Bangalore for a fortnight because of the intense heat in Delhi, and also owing to the lack of work. I don't feel inclined to write even a sentence.

The sisters from the convent phone me often. It is then that I hear of my batch mate working at Ashokapuram Hospital, Ernakulam Province, being sent away from the Congregation. Obscene scenes, spread through the internet, the CD and the mobile, have been the cause for the expulsion. What I hear about her seriously disturbs me; I can't sleep for nights, mourning over her situation. Complaining to Jesus, I ask Him: 'Why did you humiliate your own bride thus, Jesus? This is unbearable, Lord! No woman can endure this. How can a nun, dedicated to you all these twenty-six years, go through this?' She had been with us for twenty-five days at Aluva before our Silver Jubilee year. One of the sisters writes to me, 'The Mother General and the CMC have started suffering, to balance what the Congregation has done to you.' From my friend at the college, I come to know that the Principal-in-charge signs everything as 'the Principal'. As I am a gazetted officer, though on leave, I attest copies of documents of the nurses in the hostel where I am living in Delhi, with the permission of the university. As there cannot be two Principals in a college simultaneously, the matter is discussed with Fr Joseph, who asks me to make it known to the Mother Provincial-cum-Manager, officially. To my letter, not a single sentence is given as reply either through word of mouth or a letter. The Principal-in-charge is allowed to function in the same manner by the authorities. They are bold enough to violate all rules and laws. They always find loopholes, or create them in order to escape, by wielding their wand of power and wealth.

Meanwhile, a young chap named 'Agni' visits me. He happened to buy my poetry book from the Cosmo bookshop in Thrissur, and had gone to Amala to meet me. From there, he was instructed to go to St Maria's from where he got my phone number and the information that I was in Delhi. He rings me up after reaching Delhi where he has come to prepare for his Civil Service exams; he had recently finished his B.Tech. and an India tour. From him, I realize that he is the son of a classmate of mine. He finds out about a 'poetry-reading club' where we both get chances to read poems in front of appreciative audiences. For my poetry book, they pay me Rs 200, and for reading a poem, I get a gift too. Through him, I get the contact number of my former classmate and thick friend.

Fr Joseph doesn't like me in my sister's gown; he tells me either to wear saree or churidar. Saffron-coloured sarees are allowed in our Congregation as official dress, but once you change, you will have to stick to the dress. I decide to change to saree at least to please father. Getting permission from the

Provincial with great difficulty, sarees and petticoats are bought and blouses stitched. On the eve of 15 August, when I have decided to be free of my gown and veil, father asks: 'Jesme, did you change to saree of your own accord or because of my compulsion?'

'Father, after buying and telling everybody . . .'

'Forget about the money involved; did you change because you wanted to?'

This is a tricky question. Father doesn't want to own up to his persuasion. Many times, I have shared with him that personally I don't like to wear sarees. Anyway, I own up to the decision, to relieve him of his responsibility.

The inauguration of the youth ministry keeps getting postponed indefinitely. The time to do the Will of Jesus is nearing, I think. From a circular from the Provincialate, I come to know that both the Mother General and the Provincial will be together for a few days in the Provincial house. I find that to be the ideal time to act. All these days I have been absorbing grace and strength from Him. 'Arrange everything, Jesus!' I constantly pray and wait for Him to act. Meanwhile, I get Amma's consent to leave. Accepting the reality, she says, 'Memy, don't expect the family to help you again. You gave the first chance to us but we couldn't save you. Now you may get the help of your friends if Jesus so wills. I am very particular that you should do only His Will.' With her permission and blessings, I plan the details of rendering the deed. That is the first time I call Asha, my friend who has promised to help me whenever I need her. It was she who had come earlier to the Provincial house during the negotiation. What struck me then about her was her non-persuasive stand, giving utmost freedom to a person: 'Sister, I am with you in whichever decision you take. If you quit, I am there for you; if you go back, I am there, too. I am concerned about your happiness.'

I enquire if she is free in the last week of the month and get a positive answer. Next I contact my friend, a reporter, who has been keeping the ordeal I endured confidential for these eight months. Then I ring up Susmitha to get her assurance about staying at her place initially. It has been decided months ago and hence I have no doubt about it. Then I circle a date on the calendar in the last week of the month, when I should start from Delhi. But matters are not that easy. How can I reserve a ticket or pack my luggage and leave Delhi without Fr Joseph knowing? My duty is from nine in the morning to almost six-thirty or seven in the evening, including Sundays and holidays like Independence Day. With the permission of the father I can never go, as the news will reach the Provincial before I reach Kerala. They will either take me forcefully back to the convent or trick me against His Will. I contact my classmate at Delhi and get her help to reserve the ticket on the date I have settled on. Then I wait, when Jesus acts miraculously.

Father gets a call from Bangalore to do some major work of evaluation which involves his staying there for a considerable period of time. Reserving the emergency quota ticket, he is getting ready to leave. Earlier, when I was working on the questionnaire for the evaluation, he had suggested that I accompany him for this work. But, fortunately, he decides to take another father along with him and I am spared. Minutes before his departure, he gives me an amount of one lakh rupees for safekeeping. I am confused as I will be leaving Delhi very soon. How can I return the cash? Hence, I tell him that since my room is right next to the parlour, it is not safe to keep the cash there. It is a white lie, as every room has a safe with locking arrangement; but the lie is convincing.

It is then that my classmate rings me up and asks me to switch on the TV. The news of the suicide of Sr Anupa Mary and the details are being flashed by the channels. She tells me to be cautious when going to meet the Provincial and instructs me to take at least a few friends with me for support. My friend from Ernakulam calls and tells me that Jesus is creating an ideal wave in Kerala for my sake. Informing the sisters that I am leaving as the youth ministry has not yet taken off, and paying the rent to the director-father, I pack my possessions along with my letter requesting permission to leave. My classmate takes me to her flat, where I stay for a few days. Meanwhile, I get frequent phone calls from Amma expressing fear and regret at my quitting the convent. Some of my family members might have been pestering her by now. With Jesus, I proceed to the railway station and board the train.

~

The hubbub inside and outside of the train awakens me from my reverie. The train pulls in at Calicut where I should have got down. It is not as early as Susmitha had informed me. Now the train is resuming its journey. When it reaches Thrissur, I ought to be cautious. Amma might have shared my news with many and if anybody peeps into the compartment, they will certainly see me as I am the only lady passenger here. Without delay, I inform my reporter friend about my seat number and the time of the train's arrival at Thrissur. He comes there and assures me of protection and safety. Knowing the time of its arrival at Ernakulam I inform my friend, Linux, to be at the station with the porters ready near the compartment. The train arrives earlier than scheduled but he is already on the platform. Arranging a taxi, he leaves me, wishing me all the best! A hearty welcome is received at the teacher's residence.

On 31 August, as planned, I reach the KSRTC stand at Thrissur where Asha comes and takes me home. We are joined by the friend-reporter and, with my permission, Asha calls a Catholic woman who is also an ex-nun. Asha's associate and friend too accompanies us. My strict instruction to them is not to utter a word, but just be a witness to my handing over the CMC emblem and the letter requesting for Dispensation. The original letter has already been posted to the address of the Mother General. As we reach the convent, we are made to sit in the parlour waiting for the authorities. Meanwhile, a councillor comes and tries to take photos of each one of them with her mobile, despite their objection. Then another councillor comes asking me to go inside to meet the authorities. I request to allow at least one woman to come with me. But the request is not granted. Meanwhile, a former councillor rushes to the parlour with a mobile and takes photos of my companions without their noticing. I intervene and ask her not to do so. The councillor, who is my batch mate, asks: 'You have been coming inside the Provincialate all these days and now why don't you come on your own?'

'Sister, from December 6th onwards, how many times have I requested the Provincial for an interview? She has always seen me only in the presence of the councillors. This time I want to meet her with my friends.'

Finally, the councillors accept the letter, the statement of my expenditure and the CMC emblem. I inform them that I plan to apply for VRS (Voluntary Retirement Scheme) and that I don't have money to live until I get pension. 'Do you think that the Congregation won't help you financially, Jesme?' asks a councillor.

'Sister, I believe in the generosity of the CMC and that is why I remind you of it.' Returning from there, we go to Amma's, but she is about to go to attend a funeral. Like Jesus and Mother Mary meeting in the Fourth Station of the Way of the Cross, we look at each other. Next, we head towards a hotel for lunch when I get a phone call from my former chaplain: 'Is it true what I heard, Jesme?'

'Yes, Father.' He promises to call later.

While in the hotel, I get calls one after the other. From the reporters of *Deepika* and *Manorama*, the other reporters have heard about my leaving the convent. They have a battery of questions for me. Is it true what has happened? Are you branded as insane by the Congregation? If we bring a doctor to examine you, will you cooperate? I agree to cooperate. To escape from more interrogation in a public place, we hasten to Asha's house. At 3 p.m., Asha tells me that the media will reach there in half an hour and I am to face them. She emphasizes, 'Sister, now if you don't respond, only the version of the Church will be heard and believed by the public. You have a chance now to clear yourself.' Now that the Church and the CMC are indulging in public propaganda against me, I have to defend myself. They have done enough and more before, and I have been enduring the consequences till date. I would have been still within the 'religious enclosure', enduring the 'Crucifixion' until my last breath, if only they hadn't forced the psychiatric treatment upon me. Now, this is the chance given to me by my Lord, and despite my decision to ward off publicity, I shall cooperate. Anyway, I haven't called any one from the media for my self-defence.

The media saves me from the scandal spread by the Church and the Congregation. They stand together and their reports are compact and coherent. Many great people, including my former and present students and staff, ring up or come to my support in my time of trouble. And now I realize who my true friends are. The Mayor, my friend, comes offering help; my cousin brother assures help; many priests offer financial and moral support; two sisters call to console me; my own brother comes to see me; and the Vanitha Commission officially visits me. Soon after His Will has become action, I return to Ernakulam and live in a paying-guest accommodation. Meanwhile, a priest informs me that as a mediator when he talked to the CMC authorities, they said they were willing to take me back as the letter for Dispensation has not been sent yet. I object to the proposal. The next intervention is to demand my silence. When another father tells me to keep mum, I respond: 'Father, I hear sisters spreading nonsense about me. I'm scared they will create even a "blue film" on me. What can you do to keep them silent?'

'Jesme, don't you know the nature of the sisters?' he says in defence. At that point, I let myself go, 'Oh! You find it difficult to control the sisters under you; so then you try to silence the sister who has left.'

'I will talk to them about that,' he ends.

Sr Alphy, my friend, who has always supported me, wants to meet me urgently and even plans to come to my hiding place at Ernakulam. I let her know of my coming to Amma's in the course of my official visit to complete the procedures for the Voluntary Retirement Scheme. The moment she enters and sees me, she sighs: 'We live the ascetic life inside the Four Walls; you live it outside; that's the only difference I see now.' She continues: 'Jesme, there are many in the convent who love you and would like to meet you; but none has the courage to do so. Seeing you, I'm relieved of my tension.'

The Provincial informs my brother that she is willing to give me financial help, if I go to her either with Amma or him. I tell him: 'If they are willing to help me financially, let her credit to my account an amount of Rs 15,000 per month until I start getting pension.'

She readily agrees and wants a request from me to be filed. Before she tells me anything further, I have already sent the request. For almost fifteen days I wait for the money, daily asking the bank officials whether the money has been credited to my account. Instead, I get a letter from the Mother Provincial stating that, as I am to get the arrears of more than one lakh rupees, they aren't giving me the promised amount. I can very well proudly say that I have got money from the government when I am in need but not a single rupee from the Mother

Provincial. The Canonical Law speaks of 'showing charity' to the nuns who leave the nunnery. But here, that charity is denied to me, by even breaking the promise given by the authorities. When the priest representing the Bishop learns about this, he agrees that it is a shameful response on the part of the authorities. But then I hear from my own cousin that she had heard a retired office staff of St Maria's College announcing that I was getting an amount of Rs 20,000 monthly from the management. Where neither the Congregation nor the family gives a single rupee to the nuns who leave, how can they survive? None will have the financial backing or guts to file a case against the convent or the family. They will be forced to die and decay within the Four Walls.

Wild accusations do the rounds. One is that I have accepted capitation fee for seats and returned the money only when compelled by the management. Imagine! Not even a single sister will support this pronouncement. Then a professor at the neighbouring college proclaims that I have been to the film festival at Trivandrum without the permission of the Mother Provincial and I was brought back by him, and that this speeded up the decision of the authorities to oust me. What fantasies the human mind can concoct? Anyone can invent stories so long as they are not confronted by the person being targeted. I take this as an interesting outcome of the freedom which I enjoy today.

When I read the words of solace from my own students on Orkut website, I feel elated. Have my students become so mature as to be able to say that the Church is now after party politics, power and the crumbs of patronage, and so Christ is climbing down its steps and leaving? I have forsaken my position as a Principal, and thereby the gazetted status, given up my membership of CMC, and my UGC job of teaching which fetched me more than Rs 40,000 per month. This is done in order to do the Will of God and attain His Freedom and Peace. When I feel suffocated with the rawness of situations, I open up my heart to my very humane and understanding friends; then I look hard at Jesus, provoking Him, as the one responsible for all these happenings. But the next moment I relax on His lap and just thank Him for saving me from the 'Formidable Fortress' and welcoming me into His Safe Anchorage.

AFTERWORD
THE DIVINE MAJORITY

When thousands are against me but God is with me,
I definitely have the Divine Majority.

—Emerson

The Malayalam edition of *Amen*, published in February 2009, has been widely welcomed. But there are people who find it difficult to accept the truth. When the book came out, my youngest brother abused me. My family rang up Asha, who assisted me in the translation, and threatened her. Since then, they refuse to communicate with me.

Prior to the Malayalam publication, I did a piece explaining why I wrote about my experiences in the nunnery. When it came out in the monthly magazine, *Pachakuthira*, from DC Books, the Mother Provincial called and tried to dissuade me from going ahead, saying, that is what the authorities wished. I explained that the manuscript was already with the publisher and it was too late to withdraw it. Next day, two Provincial councillors visited me with the sanction to my request for

Dispensation, through a document titled 'Rescript', dated 28 October 2008, from His Grace Mar Varkey Cardinal Vithayathil, Major Archbishop of the Syro-Malabar Church. One of them requested me not to publish the book. I reminded her of my telling all concerned, that the day I left the Congregation, I would go to the media with my experiences. Furthermore, I pointed it out that in the two months since I had left, 'The CMC has not given me money for my existence; hence, I think I have to sell my books to live.' At this, the authorities offered to pay the entire amount of the proceeds from the book. Emotional means were also employed to stop me. One sister said she would sit in the chapel and recite rosaries so that all my books would be burnt away!

Even before it was launched, from the publisher's press release, many of my friends and other non-Christians came to know of the book and complimented me. Slowly, they were joined by the Christians, including the Catholics. Some priests, too, welcomed it. To my surprise, many nuns lauded my courage and proclaimed their solidarity with me, confiding they daren't write about the religious life out of fear. Many VIPs from India appreciated the book, as also many others from outside who listened to my live interview on Dubai Asianet Radio. The TV channel, Kairali telecast a popular programme, *'Veritta Kaazhchakal'* (Unique Sights), anchored by the cine actor Sri Sreeraman.

People found the book unputdownable, as one incident flowed into the other. My sincerity and courage in sharing all my experiences, unmindful of the consequences, was commended. Many also remarked they met the mystic in me.

Amen comes at an opportune moment. Recently, there has been much discussion about the findings of Fr Joy Kalliath, of the CMI, that 25 per cent of the nuns in Kerala are discontented with their consecrated lives. This has been followed by Fr Paul Thelakat's biography of Cardinal Varkey Vithayathil, *Straight From the Heart*. According to a report by Sri G. Ananthakrishnan in an English newspaper, 'The Cardinal's views have appeared in his biography, much like the nun's (Jesme) own . . . The Cardinal tells his biographer Paul Thelakat, the spokesperson of Syro-Malabar Church, that the time has come to free the nuns from the "pitiable situation they are in." I would say to a great extent our nuns are not emancipated women. They are often kept under submission by the fear of revenge by priests. That's how the priests get away with whatever humiliation they heap upon them. It is a pitiable situation from which somebody has to liberate them . . . A big complaint of our nuns is that the Diocesan priests are treating them like servants; making them wash their clothes, prepare their food, wash the church, etc. and that too without getting paid. These are all unjust ways of treating the religious women.'

Meanwhile, the attacks on me by sections of the Church continue. One issue of *Sathyadeepam*, a weekly brought out by the Church, in an article on *Amen* carries personal remarks against me and calls me 'Judas' and warns me of the consequences of my remarks. I regret that the sister who wrote that piece hasn't read the book *Othappu* (Scandal), written by Sara Joseph. She might change at least some of her observations if she had. When so many of the sisters admit the cancerous growth within the nunneries, and pray hard for renewal, how can someone shut her eyes to the harsh realities and spatter with mud those who are trying to carry the Voice of the Lord? With Jesus on the Cross, let me repeat, 'Father, forgive them; for they know not what they do.' (Luke 23:34)

The Church also brings out a bimonthly called the *Truth*. In the March issue, X, no. 2, the editor himself has done a cover story about me with the heading—'Sr Jesmeyude Aatmakadha *Amen*: Oru Vyabhicharathinte Kumbassaaram (*Amen*: The Autobiography of Sr Jesme: The Confession of a Prostitute)'. The cover carries a photograph of my body, across which are plastered my references to sex in the book, taken out of context. How low can people stoop! I should like to ask them, if they would ever dare to use verses from the Bible like 'Your two breasts are like two fawns, /Twins of a gazelle,/ That feed among the lilies,' (Canticle of Canticles 4:5) out of context and paste them over a picture of a saint?

The journal has reduced the book to three sexual events that appealed to them (there are many more references to which they are blind), and citing two of them, they brand me as a sinner. I ask, 'If I am a "harlot", how come my partner in "sin" remains inside the monastery, and occupies a high position, too, there?' Is the victim to be penalized, but the perpetrator to be applauded? The promise of Jesus that harlots and tax collectors would reach heaven sooner than the Pharisees gives me much solace. Anyhow, Jesus has come to redeem sinners; hence I am relieved to be branded a 'sinner' by the so-called 'holy' men.

I live with the consolation of support from some quarters. As I said in an email interview to *Indian Currents Weekly*, Delhi, another body of the Church, a few sisters try to keep in touch with me. Fr Paul Thelakat, in a telephonic conversation with me, affirmed the Church's solidarity with me, as he knew that I am for the Church—my *Amen* is to Jesus, to the Bible and to the Church. My Archbishop, Rt. Rev. Andrews Thazhath, told my brother when he personally met him, that as far as he is concerned, I have only quit the Congregation of Mother of Carmel but am still the loyal daughter of the Church.

I decline numerous offers either to inaugurate or preside over conventions followed by rallies arranged by anti-Christian groups and movements. I can proudly affirm, as St Teresa of Avila, that I, too, am the valiant daughter of the Church.